SOCIAL MEDIA MARKETING

2 BOOKS IN 1:
SOCIAL MEDIA MARKETING FOR BUSINESS 2019, SOCIAL MEDIA MARKETING FOR BEGINNERS

Table of Contents

Social Media Marketing for business 2019

Description 7
Introduction 9
Chapter 1 Preliminary Considerations 19
Chapter 2 Finding the Right Social Media Platform for Your Business 30
Chapter 3 Integrating Social Media into Your Omnichannel Marketing Strategy 41
Chapter 4 The Sales Conversion Process 49
Chapter 5 The Need for High-Quality Content 54
Chapter 6 How to Structure Your Social Media Team 59
Chapter 7 Facebook Marketing 66
Chapter 8 Instagram 83
Chapter 9 Twitter Marketing 96
Chapter 10 YouTube Marketing 108
Chapter 11 Flickr 118
Chapter 12 Tumblr 122
Chapter 13 Goodreads 125
Chapter 14 The Best Way to Approach Social Media Marketing 129
Conclusion 131

Social Media Marketing for beginners

Description 135

Introduction 137

Chapter 1 The Fundamentals of Social Media Marketing . 139

Chapter 2 Why my business needs social media? 151

Chapter 3 Defining your audience 157

Chapter 4 Using social media platforms for marketing ... 160

Chapter 5 Social media strategy 166

Chapter 6 The Personal Reality of Personal Branding 178

Chapter 7 Don't be too professional 185

Chapter 8 Facebook Marketing 187

Chapter 9 Instagram Marketing 216

Chapter 10 YouTube Marketing 231

Chapter 11 Snapchat Marketing 244

Chapter 12 LinkedIn 255

Chapter 13 Social Media Marketing Mistakes to Avoid ... 258

Conclusion 263

SOCIAL MEDIA MARKETING FOR BUSINESS 2019

SOCIAL MEDIA MARKETING FOR BUSINESS 2019: NEW STRATEGIES TO MAKE MONEY ONLINE AND SHAPE THE FUTURE OF YOUR SMALL OR LARGE BUSINESS CAPITALIZING ON NEW FACEBOOK AND INSTAGRAM TRENDS.

Description

Are you a business owner?

The heartbeat and pulse of every business endeavor are profits generated from increased SALES! Regardless of the nature, structure, and position of your business, one of the first things you will like to consider is finding the easiest, cheapest and fastest way to grow and steadily expand the network of your influence and customer base. The truth is, there are many marketing, income generation, and business promotion options out there, but all these have been taken over by significant technological breakthroughs of the 21st century. It is called Social Media Marketing and other Internet-based business platforms.

Do you want to drive traffic and increase sales?

Do you want to record reasonable sales in your business as much as establish your brand as the industry leader? Are you a personality that requires building a personal image online? Do you want to get the people conversing about you? Congratulations! You've found the right book: as the urge to help guide and train newbies and existing users on how to dive into this technological development inspired this.

There is a need to leverage on Internet, and social media platforms for business, passive income, marketing and promotion of your brand as social media can help you in dynamic ways beyond the capacity of traditional means of business promotion.

This book will primarily help expand your knowledge base on how businesses that care about their awareness and aim to get people conversing about them can do it as this is the first gap social media helps bridge. It brings your brand an opportunity to 'shoot your shot' at clients and thereby creating a reputation that will make you stay on the lips of users of social media and most importantly, your clients.

This guide will focus on the following:

- Preliminary Considerations
- Finding the Right Social Media Platform for Your Business
- Integrating Social Media into Your Omnichannel Marketing Strategy
- The Sales Conversion Process
- Facebook Marketing
- Instagram
- Twitter Marketing
- YouTube Marketing
- Flickr
- Tumblr
- Goodreads
- The Best Way to Approach Social Media Marketing... AND MORE!!!

Introduction

The purpose of social media for general users is fairly straightforward: you get on your chosen platform and begin to network with your friends and family. If you are looking to grow your network, you can add other people who are interested in similar things as you are and then become "digital friends" with them. In other words, you never actually meet them in person, but you share with them online on a consistent basis and get to know them through status updates, comments, and other social media conversations. It truly is about networking and, more importantly, *talking and sharing* with one another.

This is exactly what makes social media such a powerful platform for businesses to market their products on.

It has long been known that word of mouth is one of the most powerful marketing strategies at the disposal of any company. If you want to grow your business, having people share positive comments and experiences about your business while recommending you to others is a great way to start. Meanwhile, if they are sharing negative comments or bad experiences, that is a great way to end up running out of clients because people stop trusting you and, therefore, stop doing business with you. If you want to have success, then, you need to earn the positive comments and recommendations from people who have fallen in love with your business.

Since social media is already all about talking, sharing, and networking with others, it makes sense that this is an incredibly powerful platform to get on when it comes to marketing your business. People are already leveraging word of mouth; all you need to do is get on there and give them something to talk about. By creating a profile for your business and sharing content on a regular basis, you give people plenty to talk about through your profile. This way, all they need to do is engage with your business and share with others so that you are being seen by those who are most likely to purchase from you.

Because of the power of social media and the power of word of mouth, an incredible modern business has evolved from this system. That is: influencers. Becoming an influencer means taking on a business model where you are at the center of conversations, and you are the one influencing what people are talking about. Essentially, becoming an influencer means that you build your popularity on social media and then begin talking about products or services that you love, thus causing those who follow you to talk about them, too. Because you are popular and they already trust you, they are more likely to purchase these products or services.

Becoming an influencer gives you the opportunity to charge businesses for your endorsement, essentially meaning that you are paid a commission every time someone purchases something because you influenced them to. As a result, you can earn money solely through becoming popular on social media and then guiding people to purchase certain products or services through companies that are willing to pay you.

Both starting your own business giving something people to talk about or running a business where you influence people to talk about certain things, are great ways to get involved in social media marketing so that you can make a profit online. In this book, we are going to talk about how you can conquer both of these models online, allowing you to build the online business empire of your dreams, no matter what that might look like.

Choosing the Right Niche on Social Media

The first thing that you need to do when you begin to leverage social media for growing a business is find out what your niche is. A niche outlines a specific segment of your chosen industry that you are going to talk to, which is necessary if you are going to make an impact in social media marketing. Because billions of people use social media every month, and most industries are marketing to multiple millions of people, you need to have a specific segment of the market that you are talking to if you are going to be heard. Otherwise, people are going to ignore you because your information and updates do not feel personable enough for them to really relate with, connect to, and pay attention to you.

Choosing the right niche on social media is necessary regardless of where you are at in business or what business model you are using to make money online. However, there will be certain steps that you need to adjust if you are going to be developing a business online to ensure that you are choosing the niche that is going to give you the most opportunity to grow online.

If you already have a business that you have been running off of social media, choosing the right niche on social media is about finding the part of your audience that is most likely to pay attention to you in the online space. So, if your market is generally 30-40 year old women in person, you need to find out which types of women you are marketing to the most and who is spending the most time online, and then you need to focus your marketing efforts on them.

With a business already up and running, targeting your niche online is going to be incredibly simple because you already have statistics available to show you who pays the most attention to your marketing, and to your business in general. All you need to do is refine these statistics to identify who is online and what they are talking about so that you can find the right angle to talk with them online.

For example, Horace and Jasper is a leather company located in Calgary, Alberta. Their company creates belts, purses, bags, wallets, cellphone charms, wrist cuffs, and more. In reality, this company could market to just about anyone who would wear a belt or carry a wallet because of how versatile their products are. However, if they were to market to just anyone, they would not have any success in getting discovered online. Instead, they have decided to market specifically to edgy, punk rock type that is looking to shop local for products that are higher quality and backed with a more trustworthy guarantee. This way, they are speaking to a very specific segment of their possible market, which results in a massive amount of success in their marketing strategies and business growth.

Another great example of how this works is with the Honest Company. This company provides baby care and cleaning products that are cleaner, more environmentally friendly, and less harmful to your family. Ideally, they could market to anyone who lives in a house or who has young children because they are providing products that are relevant to these two segments of the market. However, they know that the people most likely to purchase their products are women who are environmentally conscious and who want to do better for their families. So, they tend to market toward women and moms who are wanting a safer alternative to harsh chemicals, which results in them having massive growth on their online platform, as well as their business in general.

Identifying your niche is less about paring down and finding one single type of person to talk to, and more about identifying the angle that you use on social media. You want to find the angle that is going to give you a specific way to talk to and share with your audience so that the ones who are most likely to purchase through you are listening and purchasing.

This is true for anyone who is just starting out in business, too. If you are starting a business with the purpose of generating success online, or if you are becoming an influencer, you are going to need to find a niche so that you know who you are talking to, why, and how to reach them. This way, you are more likely to reach those individuals.

As someone who does not already have a business in place, you do face the setback of not already having statistics around who you are most likely to earn sales from, which means that you are going to have to start from scratch. However, starting fresh means that you do have the capacity to choose the niche that is most interesting to you while also having the most growth potential online, which can be an incredible opportunity to maximize your success.

If you are brand new in business, the best thing that you can do is determine what type of business model you want to follow, and then research what the latest trends are in that particular model. So, if you want to sell products or services, you need to identify what types of products or services are selling the most online. If you want to be an influencer, you need to identify what types of influencers are making the most income online. The key here is to make sure that you are looking at the right numbers. Avoid looking at industries that have the most businesses that are online, and instead look at the industries that have the most businesses *that are actually making a strong profit* online. This is how you can ensure that you are choosing a niche that is going to be lucrative in offering you great opportunities to make money, rather than choosing a niche that is going to be saturated with businesses or influencers. If it is saturated and no one is making a decent profit, there is a good chance that you are looking at a low-quality industry.

While you look at industries that are going to offer the most opportunity, make sure that you are also looking for industries that are interesting to you. Attempting to make a go at it in an industry that you do not understand or that does not interest you is going to end with you falling flat because you are not passionate enough to really give it the type of energy it needs to grow. Instead, pick one that makes you excited because that will make it far easier to help you gain the momentum that you need to grow your business rapidly and have great success with it, too.

Creating Your Profiles and Pages Properly

Choosing your niche is only part of using social media as a marketing strategy. The next part of making the most out of social media is knowing how to set your profiles and pages up properly. Online, your profiles and pages offer a sort of "store front" for people to look at, so it is crucial that you create them in a way that helps leave a positive impression of you and your business in the eyes of your visitors.

It is important that you always approach the topic of your profiles and pages with this intention of making the best first impression possible. This way, you are looking at them with the perspective required to ensure that they are sending the right message and encouraging people to follow you, trust you, and buy from you, rather than driving people away or leaving them confused or uncertain.

Every single social media platform has fairly similar features in what is available for you to customize on your profile. Typically, you can brand your profile pictures, header images, a tagline, your username, and your wall or your personal feed. These areas can be branded to leave a very specific impression of what your business stands for so that people know as soon as they look at your profile who you are and what they can expect.

In the past, it was enough to write a basic tagline and use images that showed your logo and maybe a professional headshot of you, depending on what your industry was. These days, this type of generic approach is not nearly enough to capture the attention of people and leave them thinking about you and your services over anyone else. Instead, you need to do something that sets you apart and caters directly to your niche so that they see you, remember you, and willingly come back for more. This is where knowing your personal niche is useful: you know what type of customizations and features they would appreciate. This way, you can brand and customize your profile accordingly.

For example, if you are a realtor who focuses on the niche of first-time home buyers that are also families with children, you might make your profile picture a professional headshot where you are standing in front of a nice home that is in a family-friendly neighborhood. You may also have evidence of children in the background, such as a nearby park or playground, or some children's toys in the front yard of the home. If you are an influencer who specializes in talking to country western people who love the rodeo and western style, you might make your profile picture of you well dressed in traditional western wear standing in front of a barn or some livestock. Getting the right energy into your pictures, as well as your descriptions, usernames, and captions is crucial to really set yourself apart from other people in your industry.

Identifying Winning Strategies for Marketing On Social Media

Knowing how to authenticate your chosen marketing strategies for social media is crucial if you are going to pick strategies that are actually going to help you succeed. In this day and age, countless blog posts and articles are swirling around the internet providing all sorts of information on how you can leverage social media for business growth. Unfortunately, many of these are outdated or feature strategies that have yet to be truly tested for excellent growth. If you want to grow on social media, you are going to need to identify the strategies that help you grow *rapidly* so that you waste no time in reaching the right markets with your posts.

The best way to authenticate and validate your potential strategies is to look for other people who are using them. A strong strategy that actually works will be one that is being used by many of the major accounts, particularly those which are known for staying on top of the current trends such as brands like Nike and Sephora. Do not just focus on large brands, though, as they tend to be more resilient toward less effective strategies. Look at brands that are just a bit ahead of you as well and see if they are also using those strategies with any success. If multiple brands in all levels of success are using your ideal strategy, chances are it is a great strategy that is going to work for you, as well. If, however, you are looking at a strategy and not many people are having success with it, or it seems to be avoided or not even on the radar of larger brands, it is probably not worth your while to try it out.

In addition to looking around to see who is using these strategies and how well they are succeeding with them, you also need to authenticate the quality of the source that you have received your tips from. Receiving guidance from companies that are offering a service that is meant to help you grow, for example, may be hit or miss because they may be catering to their own services in the advice that they give. In other words, they may be giving you advice that is geared specifically toward getting you to buy or use their products to help you grow. This does not mean that it is low quality advice, or that the service being offered is low quality, but it does mean that the advice could be biased. If you are looking at strategies or advice offered by companies looking to sell their products or services to help you grow, make sure that you validate what they are saying. If what they are saying is true and is working for other people online, chances are they are a reliable source to receive information from.

You can also validate what they are saying by looking at other people who have used their products or services and seeing how their growth is going. As well, look at their own social media platforms and strategies, and see how it is working for them in particular. Unfortunately, there are many companies out there who claim to have winning growth strategies yet they themselves seem to be struggling to make any growth online. If you find that a company is making claims such as having the capacity to gain you tens of thousands of followers or earn you a specific amount of money but they themselves seem to not have that same level of success on their own platforms, be wary. These types of businesses are generally making false claims and could be offering low quality advice and ineffective services that will interrupt your success and leave you struggling.

Once you have validated the quality of your possible strategies by validating the source and validating the effectiveness of each strategy, you should be able to feel confident in whether or not these are strategies that will work. If they are not strategies that will work, or if they seem unreliable or like it may be hit or miss, avoid working with that strategy. This is likely only going to waste your time. If, however, they are strategies that are working for other people and seem to be reliable in offering growth, it is worth giving them a try to see if you can make them work for you, too!

Chapter 1 Preliminary Considerations

Before we go through the different social media marketing strategies, we have to address one thing first:

Why is Traditional Marketing Failing?

And to answer this question, we have to understand the basic concept of marketing. In essence, we create advertisements that say something about a business, have it shown in any of the channels we own or pay rent for, and then hope the advertisements draw in enough people willing to become paying customers to your brand.

And so the usual sequence for traditional marketing is always this:

Person watches or listens to something.

Advertisement butts in for thirty seconds or so to tell the person about what a business is offering.

Advertisement ends and the program resumes.

Think of traditional marketing as like a horror movie jump scare. It's something that people more or less do, not expecting to interrupt the mood, and minus the scares.

However, such form of advertising through the different online media right now is suffering from the lowest possible click-through rates and the reason is quite obvious: It's invasive, interruptive, and quite so unpredictable in its appearance that your modern potential customer gets more annoyed than intrigued.

And, given the level of control one person has with the kind of information being fed to them these days, it is not too uncommon for people to tune out from these advertisements as soon as they pop up.

According to surveys, traditional marketing has been rejected by potential audiences in a number of ways, including:

- Teenagers and young adults saying that they would unsubscribe from social media channels and websites if they feature too much forced and un-skippable advertisements.

- 86% of TV viewers immediately changing channels if advertisements start appearing.

- 91% of e-mail subscribers dropping out of their subscriptions in an e-mail list if they receive too many irrelevant notifications.

With such level of discomfort being attributed to traditional forms of advertising done in the online world, it is no surprise why they are not faring well recently.

This implies that you have to create something that would resonate well with your audience the most in any social media channel that you would wish to operate in. This means that you have to mold your message to fit the format and language of every social media site out there.

And to do that, you have to understand what makes for good marketing content.

The Anatomy of Good Advertising Content

Regardless of shape and format, advertising content would always follow the same scheme. In essence, content can come in three major categories which are:

Product - This is what the advertising is offering to the audience. It is tangible and comes in the form of a purchasable item, service, or other promotion.

Role - The advertisement basically assumes a role in your audience's life. What is it trying to do for that person? What kind of problems does it solve? What type of questions is it trying to answer? Answering these questions often determines the narrative being presented by your marketing strategies.

Emotion - An ad of this type is designed to connect to the audience on an emotional, if not personal, level. The point of this content is to evoke some kind of emotional response from your audience. Or, at the very least, it tries to introduce a new kind of perspective that could change the way they regard a certain issue or problem.

So which of these content types are the best for your business? Neither. Each has its own set of strengths and weaknesses which means that focusing on one while disregarding the others is not going to do you any favors in the long run.

For instance, focusing too much on product-based content can make your advertising feel out of touch with your audience, as they don't connect to your brand on a personal level. On the flip side, if you don't have a lot of product-based advertising and too much emotional advertising, then you are not giving your audiences something tangible to anchor their loyalty to your brand.

The anatomy of a highly effective marketing strategy in social media, then, is finding a balance between all three of these categories. Simply put, your marketing must offer something tangible, introduce something that is actionable, plays a relevant role in the lives of your target audience, and can connect to them on a personal level.

Organic and Paid Marketing: Which is Which?

A common misconception with marketing is that all types of marketing content can be lumped into a single category. The truth, however, is that marketing can fall into two categories: organic and paid.

A smart business owner would use both advertising types in tandem to reach their target market and even discover new segments in the process. However, in order to do that, you have to understand what makes both advertising types different from one another.

Organic Marketing

Marketing falling under this category is best for a number of functions including:

- Establishing the style and voice of your brand.

- Educating potential audiences.

- Driving traffic to landing pages.

- Making the business an authority in a certain topic or industry.

Simply put, organic marketing is there to increase the "awareness" for your business. The cycle of organic marketing often follows the same sequence which is:

The scheduled production and publishing of content like blog posts and articles for Search Engine Optimization

(SEO) purposes. The articles must be aligned to what your target market cares for the most, the problems that they face, and even issues that are being tackled in the wider industry that your business is a part of.

Sharing of these posts on social media. Again, the way that this content is shared must be in line with the format and language of that platform.

Tagging influencers and other appropriate brands in your social media posts as well as using your content in regular newsletters for subscribers.

Monitoring how the content is being consumed by the market. Analytics and other monitoring tools will become crucial in this phase, as it tells you whether or not people are engaging with your content and if your content is funneling traffic from your social media accounts to your main web pages.

If it is not obvious to you, organic marketing is focused on tactics that produce authentic and value-based reactions. In essence, if you produce something of value to your audience, you are convincing them more to convert into paying customers. And if you already have converted them into paying customers, the content you further produce will help in ensuring that they remain loyal to your business.

Paid Marketing

On the other hand, paid marketing is designed to help businesses optimize the sales conversion process. If organic marketing is there to "establish" your presence, then paid marketing is there to "push" it. Due to this, paid marketing is much more focused on sales and generating a purchase-focused action among target audiences.

How the paid marketing cycle goes is as follows:

Commissioning for the Creation of "Advertising Content." This would also include creating a schedule of when these ads are going to be published and in what sets.

Once the initial results are in for every published set, the marketing team then reviews which ads performed the best. Some would even invest more money in improving these top-performing ads or creating new ads similar to them.

Once every quarter is complete, the marketing team then reviews data drawn from the entire marketing campaign. Things to look for are expenses, returns of investment, returns on assets, and other important metrics.

The key to success with paid marketing is to be specific with your goals in order to produce specific actions. For instance, each paid ad might be linked to a very specific page of your website such as the landing page, the sales page, or the products page.

Other specific actions you could drive with paid advertising includes:

- Improving returns on investment and assets.

- Making a specific impression on the various platforms you operate in.

- Hitting specific sales goals or, better yet, going beyond them.

- Optimizing ads in real-time.

- Testing marketing campaigns before full implementation to identify what parts make them effective (and where they might fail).

However, the most *important* metrics you have to look out for in paid advertising will include:

Conversion Rates - The traffic coming from your social media pages that not only engage with your web pages but would actually complete the sales conversion process.

Engagement - The amount of likes, shares, views, and comments that each ad generates in a period of time after being published.

Advertisement Type - The types of advertisements that had the highest rates in conversion and engagement.

Where do These Advertising Types Fit in Your Marketing Campaign?

The one thing that you have to understand is that both paid and organic marketing actually complement each other well. There are even certain aspects where both advertisement types overlap into each other which can optimize conversion rates and incoming traffic in your main web pages.

However, the truth is that both advertisement forms are rarely used in tandem due to budget concerns. Paid advertising, as the name implies, requires you to invest more in order to generate tangible results.

On the other hand, even if you have a large advertising budget, you are not going to improve on your business's sales conversion if your content does not naturally engage with your target audience.

As such, it is important that you identify where you must use paid and organic marketing either in tandem or exclusively. Some of your marketing goals will rely on one form while others can be achieved if you used either type.

Once you have found a balance between paid and organic marketing, what you must do then is to constantly test and improve on your strategies throughout the entire campaign.

Some (Harsh) Social Media Realities That You Must Face

What you have to understand is that changes in consumer behavior has not only affected traditional marketing, but even online marketing. What worked for social media sites a few years back no longer applies today.

As such, if you want to truly survive in the world of social media, you need to face some realities about the current state of affairs.

Reality #1: Brand Recognition No Longer Means as Much as It Did

Traditional marketing has always been the act of telling the rest of the world that your business is the best of whatever it is doing or, at the very least, a fairly trusted brand in the field. But how does the rest of the social media market treat that same line whenever a company says it today? Noise. Loud, unnecessary, irrelevant noise.

The harshest truth you might face with social media is that nobody on there really cares about your business. And those that swear that they support your business won't be there for long if you start making mistakes here and there.

So, if the image you create is no longer important, what then matters for social media people? The answer is one word: solutions.

Simply put, marketing today is no longer about how well-known or trusted your brand is, but how applicable your offerings are in solving actual problems. As such, those that offer the best possible solutions to a problem, and at reasonable prices, tend to be at the top.

Reality #2: It's a Free-For-All

A few years back, the only kind of competition you needed to worry about came from the companies that offered the same products/services as you, or those that targeted the same demographics. Today, competition can come in any form or size.

In most cases, the competition you should take seriously today will come from smaller companies or lesser-known people. The reason for this is that they are closer to their target markets and can keep them engaged through a mixture of organic and paid marketing schemes (more so in the former).

In fact, you will find that less popular brands and individuals can garner stronger followings while big companies like Gap, Pepsi, and Spirit Airlines have to deal with backlash after backlash from their tone deaf social media strategies.

Also, the increase of volume in competition today gives rise to the problem of information overload for target markets. The more manufactured noise that similar companies generate on social media, the more people tend to ignore what they are trying to say.

Reality #3: Philanthropy is the New Form of Marketing

In a rather odd turn of events, marketing today has taken a rather altruistic tone. And no, this does not mean that companies have forgotten that they are capitalists by heart, as they still aim to make a lot of money from the markets.

What the shift means is that more and more people respond to marketing strategies that make them feel good. And what makes people feel good right now is if companies "stand up" for the "little man."

As such, you might notice that some companies are beginning to take up a stance in social issues, political topics, and even environmental concerns. By showing that they care for the rest of the world, companies give potential customers some value of sorts.

However, there is the drawback of becoming too political or ideological with your marketing. What you have to remember is that people don't like being talked down to. Whether it is you telling them how to live or making them feel ashamed for not caring too much, you can expect a lot of blowback from the market if the message you think is noble is perceived to be pushy and abrasive.

And there are quite a lot of brands out there that overdo it with taking a stand on social issues. The key to success, then, is to temper a business's newfound altruistic side with the notion that one is in business to give people what they want.

Either way, the point is that your brand has to give something of value if you want potential customers to trust it. Otherwise, you are not going to be as relevant in the years to come which, in turn, affects your visibility in the social media arena.

What this all means is that your marketing strategies in social media are utterly dependent on how people behave on them, whether you like it or not. And understanding the behavior of the modern day potential customer is crucial for the sole reason that, in order for your strategies to be deemed successful in social media, they must complete a step-by-step process of becoming paying customers.

Chapter 2 Finding the Right Social Media Platform for Your Business

Social media marketing is a necessity for companies that seek growth. There are many platforms to choose from when deciding on where to begin. Nevertheless, below are the three steps that can aid in locating the correct social media platform to concentrate on.

Define Your Target Audience

There may be times when you might get adverts from numerous businesses that offer services that you might not need. You understand that putting your money into that company will be wasteful. An experienced individual may then deduce that it needs to employ a person who is more competent in target advertisements.

Checking important demographics like user location and gender can help you gain knowledge about your desired audience. It is also essential to figure out the social media platforms that your competitors use to interact with their customers successfully. A simple keyword search on Google is an effective way to gain insight regarding the network that your target market makes use of the most. You can, for instance, enter terms such as golf courses + Facebook or golf clubs + Pinterest. It does not matter if your brand is the type that sticks to a particular niche; you will be pleasantly astonished at the vast array of individuals that use certain social media platforms. Interacting with a non-target audience is bound to cost money with no foreseeable upside. If deciding what target audience is best for your brand is a bit challenging, answering the questions below will shed some light on how you can achieve it.

- What are your audience's average age and gender?
- What is the average income of your prospective audience?
- What is the location of your target market?
- What companies employ these individuals?
- Do they have families?
- Are they homeowners?
- Do they face any challenges that need a solution?
- Do they have hobbies or enjoyable activities?
- What avenues do they get their information from digitally or traditionally?

When all these questions are answered, you can gain valuable insight into the demographics of your target audience.

Set an Objective That You Hope to Achieve Through Social Media

Quite a lot of business owners and social media marketers tend not to have a detailed objective to show what they want to achieve using social media. They always focus on making dreams come true without a clear definition of what their goals may be. For that reason, they often end up chasing their tails, with no visible progress in sight.

If you want to make sales using social media, it is imperative to have a clear vision and take steps towards it. You should remember that the majority of social media platforms are places where people go to view content rather than do things or be sold on things. That is why you need action to accompany your words and make money from social media marketing.

State your marketing aims for social media. Is the purpose to increase your audience, interact with current customers or enhance your brand's visibility on social media? You should audit your business by first analyzing strategies currently in place for gaps. Do you also wish to expand your consumer base, improve customer service, gain shoppers' loyalty, developing a feedback avenue, inform customers about deals, services, and products, drive traffic to your site or run an informal type of market research?

Instead of defining your aims in relation to the number of followers or fans you intend to reach, you should carefully consider the platform that will increase your level of engagement with customers. That is a metric that doesn't depict business success accurately. It is necessary to note that, on social media, a bigger audience may not always convert to money-making results.

Understand B2B or B2C Operation

Is your brand more of a business-to-consumer (B2C) or business-to-business (B2B) type?[2] The reason for this question is that it isn't common for individuals to head to digital platforms when they aim to buy something. Thus, it might take quite a bit of effort and energy to grab their attention once they are on the site.

Nevertheless, active users on social media can be the best target audience. A B2B brand is more suited to platforms that enable you to advertise and reach the correct market. One of the channels that fit the bill is LinkedIn. On this site, you can post your business information and other content that may lure potential consumers towards the brand.

A B2C brand will get a lot of opportunities through the use of social media platforms like Twitter, Facebook, YouTube, and Instagram. These are platforms that enable your brand engage directly with both your existing and potential customers.

Decide on the Content Type That You Should Create

Varying content forms are more effective on particular social media sites than others. That's why it is important to consider the format that you should create. For example, Instagram is known as an image-sharing platform, so it is wrong for a brand to choose whitepapers as an advertising tool. The proper content type is generally dependent on a few variables, such as the industry, brand, and target audience. Some of the formats that are available to businesses include podcasts, blog posts, testimonials, live streams, webinars, whitepapers, e-books, photographs, and videos.

Think of Your Resources and Skills

It is common for every channel to have a unique way of engaging the audience. However, each one also requires varying resources and skill sets to be used. Hence, you should identify what they are to create and execute a social media marketing strategy on various platforms successfully.

You must ensure that your business' needs align with a specific social media site, for one. There are a lot of marketing tools available online for free as well. These can aid in content creation and optimization for every platform. Furthermore, you should think about your strengths and research what skills and resources are necessary to remain active on such channels.

Selecting the correct platform and picking a marketing plan that fits your business is integral to save resources and time down the line.

Connect Your Audience, Goals, and Content Using the Appropriate Platform

Comparing the numerous social media sites to help you figure out which one can supply your brand's requirements the most is the next step after deciding on your goals, content type, and target audience. Below is a brief rundown of the popular platforms, what they provide, and what an average user on the platform is like:

Facebook

Facebook is the biggest networking site out there with more than 2 billion users actively using it every month.[3] As a social media platform, it is great for generating leads. It has an advertising feature as well, which can be used to customize ads for specific audiences. When it comes to building relationships, humanizing your business, and creating loyal customers from leads, Facebook is the right place to be. Like Twitter, it is capable of reaching quite a large amount of people, but it also means that you have a lot of competition here.

LinkedIn

This is the go-to option for business-to-business brands, particularly for those with lead generation as their primary goal. It is also a fantastic platform to house editorial content, which is useful for cementing your company's place as an industry leader that can be trusted to create brand value and authority while engaging leads via interactive conversations. LinkedIn has a demographic that is different from those on other sites, considering many users are typically between 30 and 49 years old.

Pinterest

When it comes to Pinterest, images are of the utmost importance. It is a great channel for entrepreneurs who intend to increase sales since many account holders make or plan purchases there. Pinterest has a more significant number of women compared to men, too, and is usually full of graphics.[4] After all, it offers creative categories such as décor, art, food, fashion, travel, wedding, et cetera that businesses may contribute to by posting beautiful photographs.

Twitter

Twitter is the type of networking site that asks users to provide rapid responses to others. It is the go-to site as well for company that wants to quickly reach followers with its announcements, breaking news, and relevant messages. The majority of Twitter users are aged under 50, and the best format to work on is textual since it can be easily digested into quotations, listicles, and how-to articles. Pictures tend to fare better on the site compared to videos as well.

Making Your Facebook Usage a Success

As one of the most used social media platforms in the world, more people understand Facebook's functionality and reach. If you are able to understand the channel's quirks, it opens up many possibilities. The question is, "Is there a way to make this platform work for you?" Below are some ways to achieve it.

Ensure That It Has a Touch of Humanity

When you personalize interactions with your followers, you can earn their trust. You have to create posts that employ a first-person, conversational tone. Page administrators have to show their names and pictures, too. When this is done, it results in increased brand loyalty as well as closer relationships.

Don't Miss Out on Using Facebook Ads

Assuming your page is not doing too poorly, it entails that your followers have grown to like your brand. You can even expand your viewership organically since your current fans are highly engaged with your content and consistently share your post with others. Nevertheless, if you aren't patient enough to wait, you may make your page more famous via advertisements.

You can get new visitors by creating sponsored stories and ads that target people who don't follow you yet. This way, you may encourage individuals with particular interests to like your brand's page.

It doesn't make sense to beat yourself up when only a paltry number of your followers see an important post. It is a reality that all business owners need to embrace. The way to combat a downfall is to promote your content more. Spend a bit of money on increasing your reach; do not get restricted by utilizing only the times your audience is online. You should see promoted posts as a way to maximize your engaged audience.

Let Your Branding Be Unique

You should offer an accustomed experience to your followers. It is essential to ensure that your page stands out from the rest. You should also make full brand information available on your profile, as well as related images and logos. It might be necessary to create bespoke features and applications that highlight your business theme, too.

Promote Interaction Between Your Customers

You have to be proficient enough to get on your consumers' good side. Customers already talk to each other, so it makes sense to take advantage of this fact to minimize costs while actively enhancing the customer experience. To be specific, highlight the contribution of loyal fans and ensure that the top contributors are recognized on your wall. This engagement can be further encouraged by creating a discussion board using Facebook's provided feature.

Find Ways to Promote Word-of-Mouth

Word of mouth is still the most effective marketing form.[5] Prospective clients tend to see fellow customers to speak more reliably about a brand than its employees or even the owner. Most people are usually swayed to make use of a service or product because a person they know has previously done it. What you need to do, therefore, is to ask current customers to share and recommend your page to others, like your posts or share your links.

Make and Mark Milestones

Looking at your brand's milestones is a great way to tell your story. Creating benchmarks helps to inform your followers how much progress your business has made. You can incorporate images to ensure these stories are much more interactive than others, too, and fans can know your humble beginnings. You can be as creative as you can with every milestone.

Have a Proper Plan for Creating and Publishing Posts

Developing a posting schedule is useful for Facebook Insights. Using this tool ensures that you can observe and schedule the best times to publish content. This is especially beneficial if your audience is in a different timezone, and you are unavailable during the particular hours when your audience expects content from you.

Using the Pin Option for Pertinent Information

An issue that most people have when using Facebook for marketing purposes is the fact that they create a post that gets only a minimal amount of visibility and ends up buried within the timeline. However, you can resolve it by sticking that content to the top of the page. Once you do so, you can ensure that the post is available right at the beginning. It lasts for as much as seven days.

Provide a Call to Action

Make sure to provide a call to action. Numerous brands tend to commit the mistake of not creating a one that seamlessly drives fans right from interacting with the page to purchasing something. Its purpose is to increase the numbers of products or services sold.

A call to action can be instantaneous but straightforward. It should be posted on the landing page and your brand's Facebook wall. You may ask your fans to register for emails or newsletters while they like and share the page as well. Current followers and prospective customers should be redirected to tabs that allow them to view products, check out exclusive deals, and avail your offerings.

Organize Contests

Organizing a contest can help you invest in your fanbase and generate publicity. For your content to run properly, it has to be actively engaged. Every moment a person enters your page's contest, a story, which their friend can view, get created. Additionally, it is essential to set it up in a manner that only current followers can participate.

Engage in Conversations

Connections can be made with prospective clients by actively encouraging interaction that goes both ways. These types of conversations increase communication, passing of information, and trust. When followers leave comments, it is important to reply to them and offer individual rewards. It is also advisable to publicly thank your followers for supporting your brand.

The moment you start a direct conversation with a customer, it actively reaches their network. Each time a follower comments on a brand's Facebook page, the conversation becomes shared among a minimum of 100 friends since an average number of friends is 338 friends for a Facebook user.[6]

Discover the beautiful work of social media for business; ensure that you are not missing out on the opportunities it offers by opening an account on a suitable social media channel.

Chapter 3 Integrating Social Media into Your Omnichannel Marketing Strategy

The advent of the internet has brought profound changes in the world today. It can be argued that the internet has given a huge boost to technological innovations. Today, there are numerous devices that people can use to purchase products over the internet. Their shopping experience is even made more convenient since they can order products from their social media pages and collect these goods from physical stores. What this means is that the shopping experience for customers has been transformed as they not only find it convenient to shop using social media apps, but they also fancy the idea that products are closer to them than ever before. Omnichannel marketing strategy centers around the idea of providing clients with a seamless and integrated shopping experience in all the marketing channels used by a particular company.

The competitive nature of businesses today should influence companies to strive and meet customer demands without bias. In this case, it doesn't matter where a customer is shopping, what matters is that they get the products that they purchased online. This means that businesses should work to seamlessly integrate both online and physical stores. For an optimal omnichannel experience, it is imperative that social platforms should also be integrated to work harmoniously. Ultimately, this leads to a huge boost in consumer engagement.

Today, we have seen businesses benefit from the fact that they are integrating social media marketing into other marketing channels that they are using. The best part is that these businesses win over the hearts and minds of their customers. In the real sense, if a customer finds it convenient to shop from their phone and get the products delivered to a physical store that they can easily access, there is a good chance that they will shop more. On the contrary, single-channel customers will not be as motivated to shop as those who have experienced the benefits of omnichannel marketing.

Digitally speaking, omnichannel customers are more proficient in the way in which they use their devices to shop. Interestingly, they are also more willing to spend compared to customers who have not been through an omnichannel experience. Often, omnichannel clients can engage anywhere and still purchase products. For that reason, it is vital that businesses should obtain and integrate insights that they get from multi-channel analytics and from their social media marketing. This is the best way to deliver exceptional customer experience that will also benefit them in the long run.

An important fact that should be made clear about the integration of omnichannel marketing with social media is that price is not a factor that influences people's shopping habits. If retailers ignore their customers and fail to place importance on their shopping experience, there is a good chance they will suffer. People will want to depend on a brand that provided them with a great shopping experience regardless of the price tags on their products/services. So, blending social media marketing with an omnichannel marketing strategy has little to do with price.

What is Omnichannel Marketing?

Maybe you are still racking your brain trying to figure out what omnichannel marketing means. This refers to a marketing approach which brings together varying communication channels used by businesses to reach their customers. Businesses use customer interests and perspectives on brands or specific products and services to optimize their marketing messages. Ultimately, this helps them to maintain consistency in all their marketing channels. The result of this is that it increases the effectiveness of marketing campaigns.

There are numerous ways in which we have enjoyed an omnichannel experience. In the banking industry, for example, there are certain banks which have taken steps to ensure that their customers can enjoy all their services from the convenience of their mobile application. In this case, you can easily schedule appointments as well as deposit a check without having to visit the bank in person. The same can be done for payment of bills and other monthly expenses.

In addition, there are loyalty programs offered by brands as a way of enticing their prospects and loyal customers. Usually, these programs are simply incentives which are meant to motivate people to purchase more of a particular product or depend on a certain service. Such exciting shopping experience gives a customer a reason to maintain their loyalty with a particular brand.

Tips to Successfully Integrate Social Media into Your Omnichannel Marketing Strategy

To guarantee that you maximize the benefits that come with blending social media into your omnichannel marketing strategy, the following points should be considered.

Engage in Social Listening

An effective way of knowing your customers on social media is by engaging in social listening. This gives you the opportunity to find out exactly where they engage with their friends on social media pages. That's not all, you will also gain insight on conversations about your industry and your brand. Analyzing the insights that you get on your customers helps you meet customer expectations as you will deliver just what they are looking for. Keeping this in mind, adding in what you learn from social listening will undeniably enhance both your products and service provision in all the marketing channels you use.

Mixing Social Media and Email Marketing

Bringing together social media and email marketing can also be a great strategy to boost engagement in your marketing campaign. How do you do this? You should consider promoting your social media pages using email. Here, you should encourage your customers to get more information about your brand by visiting your social media profiles. Remember, you should make this easy for them by adding social media buttons on the emails you send.

The same marketing strategy can also be adopted on your social media pages. Your posts should encourage people by offering them freebies once they opt to sign up for your newsletters.

Centralize the Data Collected

Social media pages provide you with a wide array of information about your customers. This means that you can make good use of this information to personalize your promotional messages. Besides knowing more about your clients' tastes and preferences, you are also informed about their hobbies, shopping habits, health perceptions, and lifestyle choices, etc.

With all the information that you get from your clients, it is crucial that you create a complete profile featuring your specific target audience. This is where the use of customer relationship management (CRM) software comes in handy. With the help of this tool, you can gather and centralize your customer information. The advantage gained here is that your social media team can work harmoniously across different social media platforms.

Never Ignore Your Audience

The last thing that you should do to your prospects is ignore them. This is something that you might be tempted to do more so when they are responding negatively to your social media posts. Ignoring these negative messages will not solve anything. It is vital that you respond to everything on your social media account. This is what engagement is all about.

Your team should be well-trained to use tools that help monitor all conversations relating to your brand. This is the best way to not miss out on anything which could tarnish your brand's image.

Support In-App Purchases

An exceptional strategy to providing your clients with an omnichannel experience is by merging your business website to your social networks. This gives your prospects and customers the ability to purchase products through their social networks. Your clients do not need to necessarily visit your business website to make purchases. Integrated links on your social media posts will automate the process for them.

Encourage Recommendations

People will want to buy your products if there are recommendations from friends in their social circle. For that reason, you should encourage testimonials from other customers who have used your product/service. Don't make it difficult for customers to tell other people about their shopping experience with your brand. Include convenient share buttons after completing transactions. This way, they will find sharing easy as they only need to make a few clicks to recommend your brand in their social circles. The same case applies if you prefer to give your customers an opportunity to leave their feedback. Aim to make the process easy for them.

Cross-Channel Social Media Marketing with Marketing Automation

Technology has indeed brought about numerous changes in the way people communicate. People always strive to be connected using social media. It is therefore not surprising to find people interacting on their social media profiles and checking their emails throughout the day. We have smartphones to help us remain connected and help us stay up to date with what is happening around us. In fact, the use of smartphones has become a norm even in the workplace and most social settings.

Businesses have to face the challenge of penetrating through all the noise and delivering their messages to their intended prospects and customers. Now, this is where cross-channel social media marketing comes in. This refers to a marketing approach where brands find an effective way of seamlessly communicating with their prospects and customers across multiple channels.

Through this marketing approach, there are several benefits that they could gain. Some of these are succinctly discussed in the following paragraphs.

Before getting into detail concerning the benefits of cross-channel social media marketing, it is important to understand that this approach is different from multi-channel marketing. Most people will confuse the two terms and therefore, it is essential that you draw a line between the two.

A multi-channel marketing approach concerns the idea of having an online presence on several channels. In this case, brands can have an online presence using a mobile application and a business website. On the contrary, a cross-channel strategy refers to an approach where brands provide their customers with a seamless experience on all the different channels that they are using to market their brand.

A good example of how this works is when customers use the internet to research brands and products that they can rely on. Often, brands will find a way of reaching these customers through email applications on their smartphones. Therefore, there is a continuous experience that a shopper will experience as brands move from one channel to another without actually interrupting the customer. Some of the pros of this form of marketing strategy include:

Increasing Engagement

Cross-channel social media marketing with marketing automation will often lead to an increase in the engagement levels between brands and their customers. The idea of using multiple marketing channels to reach customers means that you will be interacting with them throughout the day. For instance, when customers are accessing their emails and updating their social accounts. Brands remain connected with their prospects in all the stages of their purchasing cycle. Therefore, it would be easy to remind a consumer that they did not complete a particular purchase they were interested in.

Enhanced Loyalty

The consistency that a cross-channel marketing approach offers gives customers an easier way of reaching out to brands. This is because they are always kept updated with new products/services that brands are planning to introduce to the market. Discounts and other product information which could benefit them are some of the things that they are always informed about. Consequently, such interaction could drive customers to become loyal to a particular brand.

Chapter 4 The Sales Conversion Process

Although marketing might sound complicated, it actually follows a rather simple and straightforward sequence. Here's the catch, though: Any member of your audience could be in either of these stages currently.

The 4 Stages: How a Prospect Becomes a Paying Customer

You have to know in what stage of the conversion process your audience is in to craft a message that would resonate with them well. So, how does one person go from an absolute stranger to your business to a loyal customer?

They do so in 4 steps.

1. *Attraction*

Since this is the start of the process, you can expect it to be the more labor-intensive phase compared to subsequent ones. This is where any business would have to introduce people to their products/services and give them the assurance that whatever they are paying for is good.

Of course, since this is the start of the process, the target audience at this phase absolutely does not know anything about the business. As such, the goal here is to inform and educate them by answering their queries. Visibility is a major factor in this phase which is why it is recommended that you adopt a rather aggressive strategy, especially if your business is relatively new to the world of social media.

2. *Conversion*

Once your social media pages are funneling traffic to your web pages, the focus shifts from introducing them to the brand to turning them into potential leads. Here, you may have to rely on your web pages' design and even the presentation of your content to give the push that your leads need to complete the conversion process. You should also have set up systems in your pages where you can easily retarget these people at a later date.

However, your social media pages will still play a crucial role in this part. Through your channels, you can offer them something of value like discounts and promises of access to high-end content if they subscribe or register to your brand.

However, don't go straight for a "hard sell" by immediately offering them all of your available products or services, as you want them to get to know your business more first.

In other words, the goal here is to entice the leads so they would stay on your pages long enough, and make them trust you to the point that they will trade their basic information for something that they can find value with.

3. *Closing*

Once you have your leads, the goal then is to turn these people into paying customers. Since you already have their basic information, retargeting your leads should be fairly straightforward now. Once you have a pool of potential leads to your site via those subscriptions to your social media profiles, you can provide them with even better offers so they would initiate the sales process.

This can be the most demanding part of the sales conversion cycle as you are now aiming to convince people to part with their money to try out something that you are offering. The chances of people bailing on the process is quite high at this part but those that are sufficiently convinced with your marketing at this point will have increased chances of closing a deal with you.

At this point, you can only rely on the quality of your marketing strategies in the first two phases as well as the ones you are publishing at this phase. If they are quite good, people will not only initiate a transaction with the business but would actually go through the entire process, resulting in a sale.

4. *Delighting*

Most business are content with turning one visitor into a paying customer. After all, the sales conversion process is technically complete. However, it would be better if you maintain a relationship with satisfied customers.

Once the main sales process is complete, the next phase will involve enticing these customers with even more offers. The goal for your marketing at this point is to give people a reason to come back to your channels.

The reason for this is quite simple: There is no better endorser to your business than people who actually tried your offerings and found them to be good. If all of your subsequent offerings live up to the promises in your marketing, you can establish a loyal customer base which will promote your business for you in their own little ways.

Nurturing Your Leads

Let's assume that you mastered the art of converting strangers into loyal customers and you know of strategies that can quickly drum up interest for your brand. So now, you have quite a lot of traffic going from your social media pages to your main website.

However, there is still one problem that you would have to face: Not all of those visitors actually become customers. In fact, the people that actually convert into customers coming from your social media pages don't even comprise 20% of your site's day-to-day traffic.

So why aren't visitors actually making important purchasing decisions when on your social media pages? The answer is simple:

Not Everyone Who Clicks Through Your Content is Ready to Make a Purchase

You could focus on generating leads all you want. But if you want to see noticeable changes in your traffic and conversion rates, you'll have to nurture your potential leads.

One key aspect here is that you must understand that each potential lead has their own story to tell. As such, they should be handled in different ways to make them convert into customers and then free promoters.

To perform lead nurturing properly, there are a few things that you have to keep in mind:

1. Know What They Need

As was stated, not every lead is the same. Because of this, your business has to directly interact with them to understand in what phase of the conversion process they currently fall into. Have they just discovered your business?

From what social media pages did they come from? Have they filled out one of your forms or subscribed to one of your channels?

Knowing where they currently are in the conversion process will give you an idea if they are ready to try out what you are offering or not. However, just remember that just because a lead is not yet ready to make that final step towards conversion now does not mean that they won't do so in the near future.

Chapter 5 The Need for High-Quality Content

What Is a High-Quality Content?

A combination of information in a graphical, audio, written or video format that appears on a website or a page is what we refer to as content. It encompasses the sourcing and presentation of data to your audience on a specific platform as well.

The type of content that qualifies as a high-quality content will vary depending on the individual. That may talk about your products and services, photos, videos, articles, blog posts, and information pages. Nonetheless, there are certain factors that you can use to assess the quality of the content. These factors include the relevance of the content to your audience, links (internal and external), grammar, formatting, reviews, and readability.

Why Is It Important for Business Growth?

Numerous benefits are available to business owners, thanks to content creation. When creating content to publish on a page, group, or website, they can promote various products extensively, for one. The DIY content creation allows them to be flexible with the content that they upload as well.

Another critical aspect is understanding what differentiates appearance from quality. The appearance is usually essential when offering a page that is simple to use and convenient for your visitors. The likelihood that a guest will become a regular on your account is determined by the quality of content you have to offer.

Here are some criteria that you should meet before being able to claim that you got a high-quality content.

- It should not solely focus on following guidelines that will merely improve SEO rankings.
- Citing the sources should be included along with the use of valid research for credibility.
- It should have valuable information, as well as unique aspects of a website, product, service or business that you are running.
- It should undergo editing and proofreading to eliminate misspellings, typographical mistakes, and grammatical errors.
- The content should align with the expectations, needs, and wants of your audience.

The type of content and topic may lead to variations during your presentation. Regardless, the objective you intend to achieve with each content should remain the same. With a high-quality content, you can choose to have multiple objectives that allow you to improve engagement, enhance brand loyalty, and promote awareness.

When you consider the short and long-term outcomes of advertising, high-quality content is more beneficial to both your business page and websites. It often falls within a category that's known as "evergreen content" since they remain relevant even years after getting uploaded.

If you are still thinking of reasons why you need high-quality content, here are further reasons to think about now.

It Improves the Usability of Your Business Website and Page

Various factors can affect the usefulness of a site. In addition to the structure of a page or website, navigation, content accessibility, and ease of use, the content quality also matters. If you have content that has excellent internal links, it will become effortless for your users to get the information they need from your page or website.

Certain businesses cannot retain online visitors because the latter can hardly find relevant information there. The problem has to do with poor internal linking. Users want a direct link to the posts that they want to see. If they must click more than three times to find one, then you shouldn't expect them to subscribe to you.

Proper use of internal linking on high-quality content will connect different contents that contain information that your users will find relevant to the topic of interest. It is usually easier to implement if you run a blog or website for your business.

If you are writing a review on a particular product, for instance, you can add an internal link. It will redirect visitors to the main product page in case they intend to make a purchase. In an instructional article, internal linking can be an excellent way to redirect readers to the videos section of the blog or website.

In the examples above, the first use of the internal link eliminates the need for the customer to search for the product page by themselves while the second example provides a video that can the customer quickly grasp the concept you are trying to describe.

Similarly, you can link any post or video from anywhere on the internet if you feel that it will be relevant to your audience. A site that is easy to navigate and has links to relevant pages enhances usability and increases user experience. The visitors that want to share your content will also be happy to find a share button after the content. It eliminates the need for copying the URL and pasting it on another platform.

Your Customers Receive Value From the Content

Whenever you run a page or website, you always need to look for ways to outdo the competition. It doesn't matter how unsaturated the niche may be; there will still be many businesses, pages, and websites trying to win over the target audience. If you want to hold on to your viewers, you need content that provides value. That will make them interested in your business industry and may help you generate ideas. Your content will also seem valuable if it can provide relevant information and answers regarding some of the hot topics in your niche.

When your visitors start finding value when reading your content, it becomes easier for them to share it with others. In this case, you are looking for information that your audience needs and giving it to them.

It Has a Longer Lifespan

As discussed earlier, some content fall into the evergreen category. They remain relevant for months and sometimes years. With such high-quality creations, your page or website will keep attracting new visitors even if you don't post for a while.

The formats that usually become evergreen content include instructional or how-to videos, case studies, and top reviews. The topic will also play a vital role in its ability to last long.

A top-ten review of the best smartphones, for instance, will not stay in the circulation as much as an article on how to select the best smartphone. The release of new mobile devices will make the phones listed in the first article outdated as the years go by. On the other hand, the general features of a phone like the RAM size, camera, screen size, and so on remain the same. The how-to guide will show the features your customers need to assess to get the best gadget.

Creating evergreen content will not be as difficult as you may think. You can follow the steps below to create one for the first time.

- Follow the best search engine optimization (SEO) practices.
- Don't include information that is date- or event-specific. Avoid adding a timestamp as well.
- You should update content regularly.
- The content should consist of a broad range of topics relating to the industry in its discussion.
- You should provide value and eliminate grammatical errors.

Although evergreen content is quite beneficial, you need to achieve a balance when posting them. While a review may not remain useful for a long time, it still falls within the expectations and needs of your customers. Striking the right balance will attract new people and keep your audience coming back.

Chapter 6 How to Structure Your Social Media Team

With over 2 billion people active on social media, it shows that your business stands to benefit by having an active social media presence. Social media channels including Facebook, Instagram, Twitter, LinkedIn, YouTube, and Snapchat provide you with a wide market to target in your marketing campaign. Marketing your brand on these social media pages isn't just about posting content and responding to your followers. Besides posting information to these accounts, you also need to manage your marketing campaign. This entails knowing what to post and the right platforms to use. More importantly, it also centers around working with the right social media team.

The structure of your social media team will have an impact on your business' success or failure. This section takes a look at some of the most important considerations when structuring your team.

Evaluate Your Current Situation

A crucial step that you ought to take before doing anything else is to ponder on your current situation. This is because there are a number of factors which will have an impact on the decisions you will be making. Your budget, for example, will influence the number of people you will choose to hire. Additionally, this will affect the social media marketing tools that you will utilize.

You should also spend some time evaluating the team that you currently have. A small company will want to cut on its overcall costs by using their current team if they are qualified to handle certain tasks. What's more, going over the resources that you can use in your marketing campaign can help a lot in knowing what you need to successfully conduct a marketing campaign.

Creating a Social Media Governance Board

You will want to have a team of professionals capable of delivering their best concerning the social media marketing project at hand. In addition to this, you should think about creating a governance board. This is a board which comprises of stakeholders and executives who oversee the whole marketing campaign. Their job is to make sure that everything runs smoothly and according to the company's goals. In your absence, they should provide directives to ensure that challenging situations are properly dealt with.

The following are pointers to help you in creating a social media governance board.

Determining the Governance Members

The first step towards creating a social media governance board is to determine who you want to serve here. Regardless of the fact that you might have people who are qualified in various ways, it doesn't guarantee that they are the right fit. Your selection should be based on key people in your social media marketing strategy. The main thing that you will be looking for here is people with the ability to foster the right direction in your marketing campaign. Some individuals you can include here are content managers, executives, directors, etc.

Create a Board Charter

After coming up with a list of people who will be serving in the governance board, your next move should be to schedule a meeting with them. During this meeting, you should discuss the goals and missions of the governance board. The outcome of your meeting would be the creation of fundamental principles that govern this board. Roles and responsibilities should also be a topic of discussion in this meeting. Generally, the significance of this meeting is to make sure that every board member knows what they should do to enhance productivity in your company.

Clarify Social Media Goals

Once the board members are made aware of their respective duties and responsibilities, the next thing is to clarify strategic social media goals. Here, the focus will be on determining the current social performance of the company and the marketing direction that it will be taking.

Break up the Project into Stages

There are varying social media marketing techniques that companies can use to reach their goals. Nonetheless, it is a prudent idea to breakdown the process into stages. The significance of this strategy is that it makes the marketing campaign easy to handle. So, instead of posting content on various social networks, it is a brilliant idea to divide the whole marketing campaign into stages.

Communicating Goals and Training Staff

The governance board is responsible for communicating the social media goals to training staff on how the set goals can be achieved. As the business owner, you should be there to meet with the board members and discuss more on the social media goals. You want to be on the same page with these stakeholders which means that your presence is of great importance.

Once you are sure that your governance board is ready, the next thing should be to communicate to the rest of your social media team. Other employees should also be trained on how they will be operating. This includes knowing where they should seek clarification whenever they feel stuck.

Your governance board should not forget the importance of meeting regularly to evaluate the company's progress with regard to set goals. Depending on the size of your team, these meetings can be scheduled weekly or monthly.

Staffing Considerations

There is a lot to consider when creating your social media team. Most new social media marketers will jump to the conclusion that one should only take into consideration the qualifications of your new team members. While this is an important factor to think about, it is not the only thing that you will be examining when putting together your social media team. Other factors that will influence your staffing are discussed below.

Budget for New Employees

Your new staff budget will definitely affect the number of people that you will be recruiting. If you are running on a tight budget, you will have to settle for a few employees capable of meeting your social media goals.

You should never focus on looking for cheaper hires because of the limited budget you have. Undeniably, this will only push you to settle for less. Moreover, it increases the likelihood of going for the wrong people. Therefore, strive to hire fewer people who are qualified instead of trying to save money by looking for people who are underqualified.

Strategic Goals

The strategic goals of your social media campaign will have a huge impact on the people you will be choosing to work on your social media campaign team. In most cases, this will affect your team's size. The bigger the goals you are looking to accomplish, the bigger your team should be. Moreover, if your company places high regard for the importance of social media marketing, then there is a good chance that you will want a big team.

Skills Required

When choosing members for your social media team, you should consider the skills that you are looking for in your marketing team. Some of the positions that you should fill when making your team selection include:

- Social Media Manager

An individual taking on this role will be responsible for creating a social media marketing strategy. For a small company, a social media manager will take on most of the responsibilities regarding social media including coordinating social media accounts, social listening, publishing content, and responding to comments.

- Content Creators

Content creators will also form an integral part of your social media team. These are the people who will work to make sure that content posted resonates with your target audience. In addition, their responsibility will be to deliver quality content that could easily encourage the audience to like, share, or retweet. Considering the fact that content is king in your social media campaign, you shouldn't ignore the importance of hiring content creators.

- Community Manager

Another crucial member of your team will be the community manager. The role of this person is to engage with your target audience. This means that they should be there to resolve any negative publicity related to your brand. Their efforts will be required to make certain that social media engagement is given a boost.

- Analyst

Evaluating your social media performance will contribute a lot to the success of your business. Often, this is made possible by using performance metrics such as traffic, engagement rates, conversions, shares etc. If you lack the required skills to track and understand how performance can be improved, then you should not forget to hire someone to do the job.

Social Media Platforms to be Used

Once you have determined the people that you will be working with, you should also take a moment to think about the platforms that you will be using. Certainly, there are tons of social media networks out there. It is crucial that you settle for the best fit for your business.

In line with choosing the most appropriate platform for your business demands, marketers might end up concluding that they should have more members to oversee different social media accounts. Sure, this might appear as a desirable move. However, there are problems that you could face including collaboration issues and consistency in your brand's voice. Accordingly, hiring more people to help you manage the different social media profiles you have is not always a wise strategy.

Fortunately, there are several social media management applications which can be used to reduce the management workload by bringing together social media profiles on one platform.

Content Strategy

The content strategy that you will adopt will also have an impact on your staffing decisions. If you are going to create high-quality content, it means that you will have to consider hiring experts for the job. Creation of videos, for example, is quite demanding. If you don't have the required skills to create interesting videos, then it is likely that people will not like your content. Therefore, as part of creating a good social media team, you have to hire skilled individuals to create the quality content that you are looking for.

Choosing the structure of your social media team will depend a lot on what you think works for your company. Regardless, there are a number of responsibilities that you should remember to cover. First, your social media team should align with the company's overall goals. It is also vital that you clarify the social media marketing objectives with your team. That's not all - social channel optimization and the content strategy to be utilized should be clearly defined for the team to work effectively. Without a plan, it will be difficult for you to coordinate campaign activities meant to promote your brand on social media. More importantly, social analytics will come in handy as they ensure that you know whether you are performing well or not.

Chapter 7 Facebook Marketing

Facebook is made for one thing — influencing people to buy your brand, and subsequently, your product. What you sell on Facebook is not your product, but your brand. Your brand is everything that is built around your product — the kind of service, connection to the brand and company name, and the lifestyle you want to portray. People don't buy products anymore simply out of usefulness; they buy products that can add to their sense of being. So, what you need to sell to people are the lifestyle they associate with the product. If buying a product will make them feel like they're part of a trend or, say, helping the environment, they are more likely to engage with your brand. When people look to buy an expensive bag or perfume, what they expect along with it is a luxurious buying experience that makes them feel fancy and cared for.

Of course, not everyone can just open an expensive store and serve champagne to make people feel like, in buying this product, they are buying an entryway into a more prestigious lifestyle. What you can do, though, is create a similar experience through Facebook — which allows you to not only connect with your users on a personal level, but also to study their interests and likes to develop your product experience accordingly. In a way, Facebook is better for selling than regular shops, because of the constant communication and feedback between the customer and the seller. What you need to do to extend the reach of your product is to take this opportunity to study your customer base and create a Facebook Page that not only attracts customers because of the product, but because of brand association.

Brand association and its creation through Facebook is invaluable for your business, because products are replaceable. Perhaps somebody else is selling the same thing, and maybe even at a cheaper rate. The only way to gain a competitive advantage in such a situation is to make people feel more included in your selling process. People buy on the basis of trust, so you must personalize yourself for them.

Showing that you care about the community you are selling in, along with creating relatability by latching on to ongoing trends and culture, is the best way to make people feel that they should exclusively buy your product. It is no secret that Facebook is the most popular social networking website in the world. Over the years, Facebook managed to evolve into an advertising tool for companies, and now plays host to several businesses that use it as a platform to promote their business. Facebook for business is now not just a fad, but a very lucrative concept that more and more companies are identifying with, and incorporating, to avail multiple benefits.

On the face of it, social media marketing is mostly free. However, it takes a sizeable amount of effort to learn how to make the most of this free tool. Of course, that's why this book is so necessary.

Basics Skills for Facebook Marketing

Although most business owners have heard about the powerful effects of social media marketing, few are confident in using it to benefit their businesses. Facebook is not designed to automatically lead you down the path of profitability. No, you need to discover that knowledge yourself. I can help you understand what to post and how to post it in order to move your fans to buy your products. Along the line, you'll learn some key skills that will help your business gain traction in the marketplace. Here are some basics skills that outline everything you need to know about Facebook marketing:

Complete and long-term commitment to Facebook marketing:

The more you understand about how social media marketing works, the easier it will be to commit to using it. And this is a long-term commitment; you don't immediately arrive with a fully-developed Facebook marketing campaign, replete with a page that has a huge, vocal following that draws in and converts customers. It's a continual process involving ongoing self-education. You'll be actively tweaking your marketing approach to stay up-to-date with trends and to take advantage of current events. The Facebook application itself is continually evolving, adding functionality that a savvy marketer can take advantage of to keep one's business on the cutting edge of success.

Understand how social media marketing works:

You'll want to learn how basic marketing principles apply to social media marketing. You'll be discovering how you can implement effective strategies to build a successful Facebook marketing campaign. This goes far beyond just setting up a profile, presenting product images with attractive descriptions, and hoping people find your new site. You'll be discovering some specific strategies used by successful Facebook marketers and learning how to apply them to your business situation.

Turn your fans and followers into loyal customers:

Regardless of how many followers or fans a business has, it doesn't automatically translate into sales. You'll be discovering skills that will help you transform interested individuals into loyal customers.

Understanding the psychology behind buyer behavior:

You'll need to learn what lies behind a customer's decision to buy a product or service. Armed with this knowledge, you can more easily design effective marketing campaigns on Facebook.

Set clear goals for marketing on Facebook:

As you gain a clear image of what can be accomplished through social media marketing, you will be able to establish specific objectives for what you want to see happen and apply practical marketing strategies to get you there.

Learn to capture and convert leads:

Discover what leads look like on Facebook and how you can trap and develop them into paying customers.

Establish reasonable expectations:

Discover what Facebook can and cannot do for you. Learn how to incorporate Facebook marketing activities into your daily routine, as well as your future planning activities.

Learn how to attract the right audience:

With any business, your marketing plan involves knowing your target audience and how to reach it. Once you know these basic principles, you then need to learn how to apply them to the medium of Facebook.

Know how to get a bigger audience:

Most businesses need a sizeable audience to make any type of impact. While engagement is important, that engagement comes from your pool of followers. You'll need to know how to increase the size of this pool to boost the amount of engagement.

Learn to function proactively:

You can't just assume that visitors to your site will press the "like" or "follow" button. Unfortunately, this rarely happens. Learn how to give your visitors a good reason to follow your business.

Learn what to promote:

Social media marketing is not about pushing products; it's about developing trust. Learn how to shift your focus to trust building, and you'll end up selling more products.

Learn how to post effectively:

This can be a little tricky. If you post too frequently, you'll annoy your followers or even be classified as spam. If you post too seldom, you'll not be seen at all. You also need to know what kind of content is most helpful to post and what to stay away from.

The purpose of this section is to help you understand how Facebook works, how Facebook for Business works, and the wonderful things you can do with the platform to reach out to potential buyers and influence them into purchasing your products or services.

Facebook Apps

Facebook is also available on mobile, and can easily be downloaded from the app store. The user interface is extremely friendly and will help you navigate through the different aspects of a typical page. Most people prefer to check the news feed available to them on their homepage and remain updated with the various developments.

Facebook has a number of applications that can be useful for anyone running a social media business portfolio. These applications were made for the sole reason of helping businesses create a strong social media presence.

Facebook Groups is one such application. You can create a Facebook group for your product, business, or just your staff. The main purpose of this application is to manage groups easily; it can be slightly difficult to manage multiple groups. You can review all the posts and interact with the members, and you don't have to open your Facebook app every time for this. Further, you can sort out the notifications for groups because groups tend to spam a lot; this way, you can keep your Facebook id and group-related business separate.

The second app is called Facebook Page Manager — a must for anyone trying to increase the reach of his or her page. Managing a page is not simple and requires a lot of work; it can be hard to deal with page-related issues on the regular app. Page Manager has a brilliant and easy-to-use interface that is perfect for anyone managing a page from their phone. It allows you to customize your page, adjust settings, or address many other issues from your phone, meaning with this app, you can work on the go.

Apps for Business Marketing

There are various apps that every Facebook marketer must have in order to be more successful. These apps are not officially made by Facebook but are meant to help you in running a business page on the platform by providing help with the content on your page and even with tracking progress.

These apps are fairly straightforward, and they are a must-have for anyone who is running the Facebook page for a business.

Custom Tab Apps

These are the kind of apps that help you to install a small website on your Facebook page. You can have customized videos, images, and other content on a single tab with the help of these apps. Not everybody has brilliant editing and computer skills; if you are one of those people, these apps will do that work for you, allowing you to offer your customers everything that they might need. Recommendations: Hayo and Tabsite.

Email capture apps

These are the apps that will help you capture the email addresses of your Facebook audience without disturbing them. It can be really difficult to get email addresses out of people, and you need these email addresses because it expands your reach. You can get the email address from the people who visit your page by guiding them to click on certain links, so you don't have to ask for email addresses directly. Recommendations: Constant Contact and aWeber.

Quiz and Poll apps

These are the kind of apps that help in preparing polls and surveys to post on your page. Quizzes and polls are an important way to gain customer feedback; the more customer feedback you have, the better you can serve your customers. You need apps for this purpose because it's really difficult to get people interested in taking a short survey or quiz. Quiz and poll apps ensure that whatever you create is viable enough to attract people easily. Recommendations: Woobox and Antavo.

Automatic Posting apps

These are the apps that can be a life-saver for anyone who does not have the time to regularly update the Facebook page of their business. Automatic Posting allows you to create a post now and then schedule when you want that post to publish. The post will appear on your page automatically at the time that you set. This is really helpful because not everyone has the time to regularly post stuff on his or her page, but if you don't post stuff, your page starts to look dead. This gives a very bad impression to any customer who visits. Scheduled posting ensures that your page seems active even when you are too busy to post anything. This can be done directly on Facebook itself, or there are apps that will do it for you. Recommendations: Buffer and Rignite.

Social Media Integration apps

Social media integration is the concept of being able to use different social media sites with the help of just one app. By using these apps, you can connect different social media sites to your Facebook page, so that whatever you post on other social media sites also appears on your Facebook page. So, if you post something on your Twitter or your Instagram, it will automatically be posted to your Facebook page with the help of Social Media Integration apps. You get a lot of benefit out of this because many users follow a couple of social media sites exclusively, these users might just get connected with you on other social media platforms if they see your Facebook posts. Recommendations: Pagemodo and Tabsite.

Contest apps

Contests apps help you to organize contests on your Facebook page to increase participation in your business and keep your audience interested. Contests can be difficult to organize and take a lot of work; you even have to check the terms and conditions that Facebook has laid out for organizing contests. You can deal with all of this with the help of Contest apps because they make it easier for you to organize a contest, and they make sure that you comply with the terms and conditions of Facebook. Recommendations: Offerpop and Votigo.

Facebook Marketing

Facebook is one of the most innovative markets to use to sell your products. If you correctly tap into the platform's potential, then you will definitely be able to successfully market your products. Facebook Marketing is based on trying to capture the imagination of your audience in new and interesting ways. If you can get your audience to relate to your product, you'll be able to sell it to them.

If you have an established audience, you can definitely use Facebook to influence people so as to create a positive attitude toward your products. A lot of companies are using this strategy; they actually hire Social Media managers — people who are exceptional at handling social media platforms in order to create a positive image for the product and increase its reach. You can do all of this by yourself, however — all you have to do is understand how important Facebook is, set up your page correctly, and understand how advertising works.

Facebook is especially important for small businesses. These businesses do not have a lot of money to invest in expensive advertising campaigns. They can use Facebook to create a fan following for their products and generate enough awareness and revenue to get to that level where you can afford those expensive advertising campaigns.

Creating Facebook Business Groups

Being able to build up an online community is going to be one of the most important steps to make your business grow. It's going to help you get in touch with your key demographic. Building a Facebook page is great because it can help bring new customers to you. But, what about your existing customers? A Facebook group is going to be a great way for you to keep your existing customers in the loop. Not only that, but you'll also will have the ability to convert those that are, "just looking" into customers that are coming back for more every month!

How to Create a Facebook Group

You most likely have already created a Facebook group before. But, just in case you haven't, let's go through the steps on how to create one so that it doesn't seem so intimidating.

1. Enter the URL Facebook.com/groups into your search bar. This is going to take you directly to the

set-up page so that you don't have to search through pages to find what you're looking for.

2. Click on the button that says, "create group". This can be found in the top right-hand side of the page. From there you're going to be asked what your groups goal is.

Tip: It's advised that you pick the, "connect and share" button as your goal so that you're able to keep in contact with your members, and provide ongoing support so that they continue to come back for more.

3. Enter your group name. You're going to need to name your group, and while you do that, make sure that you're naming it something that your customers will remember and mentions the name of your business.

4. Invite members to your group! Invite existing customers to your group because they will interact with you, and because you know that they have an interest in your business.

Tip: Try to avoid adding potential customers until you've completely set the group up!

5. Set up the privacy settings. Make sure that you're not putting your group in a setting that you don't want it to be in. Open groups will be open to the public, which means that everyone can see what is posted in the group and who is in the group. Closed groups can be found by anyone on Facebook but the only people who can see what is posted will be members. Secret groups are just that, secret! The only people who can view the

group's content or members will be those that have been invited to it.

6. Enter your group's description. Those that already follow your business know what your company is, but why are you creating a Facebook group? Make sure that you put a description that will tell your members exactly what to expect from the group. You'll also need to choose a cover photo for your group, make sure that your cover picture is reflecting your business properly. It's a good idea to create an image that is going to make the group appear inviting while also featuring your brand.

7. Promote your group so that others can join.

g. One way that you can promote your group is to advertise it in your newsletters and correspondence that you have with your members already.

h. Post it on your business page that you just created, and pin it to the top of the page so others can always see it.

i. If you have the budget, use boosts in order to promote your posts about the group.

j. Invite people who will be interested in your group.

What's Next?

So, now that you have your group up and going and you've gotten some members, what are you going to do next to ensure that your group continues to stay active, and you're able to engage your members?

1. Post regularly: You should post hot industry topics that your audience will appreciate being made aware of. Never make them feel like they can't ask you questions, because when questions are asked, this is going to guarantee engagement boosts while other users put their answers in the comments.

2. Share something other than your own content: When you share articles and updates that are not about your business, your group is going to see you as authentic and an authoritative source of information.

3. Use Facebook Features: Take advantage of Facebook Live so that your customers can see the real you and know that it's someone that they can trust. This is also a great time to host a Q&A, or provide your group with exclusive insights.

4. Use ads in order to promote your group: Paid ads will be set so that they are suggested for those in your intended demographic. When you attract more members, you're going to have a better chance to widen your fan base.

Using the Facebook Business Manager

You've set up your Facebook page and your business group so, what are you going to do now? Now you should look into using Facebook's Business Manager. Facebook business manager gives you the following opportunities:

1. Work with a social agency or social media manager that will help by monitoring the quality

of what is being done and keep tabs on the work that is being done for you.

2. You'll have the opportunity to have multiple accounts for your business in one place.

3. You can delegate roles and tasks to your team members so that they get done, and not everything is on you.

However, that is not the only thing that you have the ability to do with Facebook's Business Manager. This tool is 100% free and very secure, and keeps you in charge by allowing you to delegate tasks without having to share your personal Facebook with your business page.

In the end, Facebook business manager is going to make managing your business more professional.

Why You Should Use Facebook Business Manager
So, the first thing that is probably going through your head is why should you be using Facebook's Business Manager when you feel that you're delegating tasks and managing your business just fine on your own.

First, Facebook's Business Manager is going to help you gain access to your pages and different ad accounts so that different roles can be established, and tasks can be assigned to those that are working inside of your business. Even if you're a small business right now, you never know when your business will boom causing you to need help, which adds to why you should allow your team members to be able to access your business page to do the tasks that you send to them. Do not fret, as a business owner, you'll still have full control over giving permission and revoking access to people.

On top of this, it's going to allow you to keep your business pages from mixing with your personal pages so that it's a lot less awkward, and you're not accidentally posting something to your page that shouldn't be there.

Let's not forget to mention again, Facebook's Business Manager is free!

Setting Up An Account

Just as setting up your business and page were, setting up an account with the Facebook's Business Manager is easy too! Let's walk through this process together so you can get through it simply and fast.

1. Ensure that you'll be able to confirm your identity with your personal Facebook page. You need to make sure to have at least one business page as well as have an ad account that can be transferred over to business manager.

From there you're going to be able to sign up for Business Manager. Enter business.facebook.com into your search bar and once the page pops up, click on create account. Here you'll need to enter all the details for your business so that everything can be transferred over from your Facebook to your business manager.

Note: It's highly recommended to have a minimum of 2 admins for your business manager account so that the page isn't placed on just one person. This is also going to keep people from locking others out of the page in the event that a conflict arises.

2. Connect your ad account. You'll now need to connect your ad account using the following steps.

k. Click on the ad accounts on the left-hand side of your screen.

l. Choose the button that says claim an ad account in the event that you already have one.

m. However, if you're new to ad accounts you need to create one by choosing the third option on your drop-down menu.

3. Next you'll delegate the roles to employees and assign tasks throughout the account. The page admin is of course going to be at the top of the food chain and is going to be the only one who can assign tasks. From there, the managers will be able to complete the tasks that you give them, but they are not going to have full access to your page.

To be able to add a new manager you'll click settings and then pick the button that says people on the left sidebar before you move on to adding a new person.

Note: You're going to have the ability to add new managers through their business emails, but they will still be required to verify their account through a personal email.

4. Delegate tasks! Now that your managers have been added, you'll be ready to start delegating page tasks. Here's how you can do that.

n. Select pages or ad accounts. The button that you click is going to depend on what kind of task you're assigning.

o. Choose the page or account that you're granting the manager access to.

p. Next, click on, "add people" and select the managers who will be granted access to have the option of completing tasks

Next you'll have the option to assign tasks such as posting, moderating comments, managing ads, and whatever else you need to be done.

Congratulations, you have set up your Facebook Business Manager account! Once you have gone through these four simple steps, you're now ready to master Facebook Business Manager. If you still find that you need help, Facebook Business Manager offers a FAQ that will troubleshoot all of the common issues you may be facing.

Less Stress But More Control

Thanks to this tool, you're no longer going to need to worry about handling every aspect of your business because you'll have the option of handing it over to people who you trust, know what they are doing; or you may hand it over to hired social media help.

Now you'll have more time, which allows you to focus on other facets of your business so you can grow it bigger! You're a business owner, you deserve to be thinking of the bigger picture rather than being bogged down by the daily details that will lead up to that bigger picture.

Chapter 8 Instagram

Instagram is a terrific platform for building your brand. This is especially true for certain ecommerce niches like fashion and lifestyle, but not so much for others, which is why we will keep the discussion on Instagram short. Service-based brands cannot always be portrayed as effectively as products on Instagram. On the other hand, if you're building an e-commerce-based brand, then this chapter will be vital to your social media marketing efforts to showcase your brand and wow hundreds of thousands of people.

Instagram is a visual platform, so the stories and content that you will be preparing for Instagram have to be highly image-based by nature. Instagram is chock full of online shoppers who are looking for a more streamlined newsfeed based on images rather than Facebook; this is a fact that most e-commerce businesses utilize to their full advantage. Instagram also boasts a higher audience engagement rate than Facebook, which is another big plus for social media marketing in 2019. Combining the engagement rates with the fact that most of Instagram's audience is actively looking to buy something, successful marketing campaigns on the platform can and will lead to substantially higher conversion rates in sales numbers for your brand than Facebook. The only problem is that, while Facebook's algorithm can be somewhat predictable, Instagram's is a lot like Google — unpredictable and ever-changing based on factors that move up and down with each algorithm update.

Strategies for Instagram Marketing
To run successful social media marketing campaigns on Instagram, here are a few things that you should keep in mind:

Update New Posts

Frequently update with new posts so your brand presence doesn't get pushed back by others. This means constantly creating new image-based content for your brand's newsfeed. Like Google and Facebook, Instagram also employs machine learning and AI to streamline your audience's newsfeed, so make sure your posts share relevant themes to appear constantly.

Use Images and Videos

Videos are also an important part of Instagram now, especially stories. The video duration for Instagram stories are very short, so it's best that you create a storyboard to make a structured narrative for your stories. If you have a minimum following of 10,000 people on Instagram, don't forget to add links to your stories. When Instagram stories were first launched, only big brands could add links to story posts, but now any brand entity with the above-mentioned following can add website links to stories, increasing the chance of driving traffic to your website for sales conversions.

Create Viable Marketing Strategies

Introduce viable marketing strategies that will encourage your Instagram followers to tag you in their stories. This will ensure that you constantly stay on their newsfeed, as well. On the flip side, you should also publish user-generated content that is relevant to the theme of your brand to gain bigger outreach. Unlike Facebook and Webmaster outreach methods, which require good communication skills to make the other party agree to share your posts and content, this happens naturally. Additionally, your audience feels special, making this a great technique for an increased audience outreach that is gained organically (without any paid promotion).

Use Social Influencers

Don't underestimate the power of influencers on Instagram, as they are the segment of the Instagram population that keeps the social media marketing ball rolling. To run successful social media marketing campaigns on Instagram, you need to have the best and most followed influencers within your reach. Now, there's one catch to this — hiring influencers to promote your brand can be very expensive, so you'd better have a fat wad of cash in order to hire one. Alternatively, you can provide them with free products from your brand in exchange for showcasing them, which is a tactic that works well with influencers who have a small or medium audience reach. Bigger brands often offer perks like paid vacations and photo-shoots, which can also bring down payments made to influencers. When choosing influencers, pick the ones who showcase their daily lifestyle while promoting brands, since they come off as more genuine, in turn, making the audience feel that the brand represents their regular lifestyle. Different types of influencers are suited for different kinds of promotions. An influencer specializing in luxury brands will not be effective for your marketing campaign if you're promoting non-luxury products that can be termed as average.

Show Your Instagram

Since SEO for Instagram is a bad idea in general, one thing you can do is show your brand's Instagram profile on a search engine by using Google's schema.org markup. Not only should you do this for Instagram, but you should use it for all other social media profiles of your brand on other platforms, as well, such as Facebook, Twitter, and LinkedIn.

Provide a Rich Bio

Providing a rich bio for your Instagram profile is crucial for audience outreach. Include the core keywords you have chosen for your search engine rankings in the same way you would for meta-descriptions. The bio is the only HTML-rendered element on Instagram that can be crawled by search engine bots, so this is the only valid SEO optimization you can do for your Instagram profile. Also, don't forget to add a link to the main website on your Instagram profile, though it comes with a no-follow tag by default — something is better than nothing, right? You should also add email addresses, as this has started to become standard practice when setting up Instagram profiles.

Focus On Your Profile Design

Focus on your profile design when setting up your account. Unlike Facebook, where you can have different types of content to keep the audience engaged, Instagram is all about looking good. If your profile doesn't look good, then don't expect high levels of audience engagement in your marketing efforts. Your image content should have a consistent design and editing style that will make it stand out from other brands.

Use Instagram Stories

If you can afford it, cover your brand's launch via carousels and Instagram stories. Carousels allow you to place multiple pictures one after another to form a structured narrative without appearing spammy.

Use Instagram Live-Stream

Similar to Facebook's live-video streaming option, Instagram also added a similar attribute last year as one of its platform features, though it has mostly gone unnoticed by many small- and medium-scale brands. If you're confident that you can create an attractive Live-Stream event, go ahead and do so — you will be capitalizing on something most businesses aren't. While you're at it, you can also invite influencers to take part in your live broadcasts. Some ideas for using the video live stream feature of Instagram include product launches, expert roundups, and exclusive short-term promotional campaigns that only dedicated audiences can capitalize on.

Create A Mini Video Channel

Do you wish to create your own mini video channel on Instagram, without using YouTube or Vimeo as the server platform? If so, you should consider using Instagram's IGTV feature. This was also introduced to Instagram last year, and unlike the video live streaming feature, it has generated a lot of buzz among the brands that are on Instagram, both big and small. IGTV can host videos ranging from ten minutes to an hour, depending on whether your brand profile is verified.

Dos and Don'ts

Here are some important dos and don'ts to keep in mind when putting your social media branding efforts into Instagram:

- Don't try to optimize Instagram posts for SEO. It is extremely difficult to index and rank, and even if you manage to accomplish this extremely difficult task, that

SEO effort will vanish with the next Instagram algorithm change. Instead, keep an eye on Instagram insights and modify your posts accordingly to increase your outreach.

- Try to maintain an even flow when sharing posts on Instagram. If your followers are constantly flooded with your posts on their feed, it will boomerang back on you and possibly lead them to unsubscribe from your Instagram page.

- Buying followers might be a tempting way to gain access to some of the more premium features of Instagram, but don't do it. What will happen is that, like many failed business pages on Facebook, you will end up having a lot of followers with little to no engagement, which will raise red flags to potential real followers who could have been successfully converted into a sales opportunity.

- Avoid posting adult content on your Instagram posts or stories, as this will likely turn off a lot of potential followers and lead to drops in engagement ratios.

- Stick to regular marketing and promotional campaigns, but don't be too pushy. If you come off as trying too hard or create a needy image, your followers will start to doubt your brand and the quality of the products you're offering.

Don't go crazy with your hashtags. Sure, they're your primary means of connecting with audiences and letting your audience engage others with your posts, but excessive use of hashtags often backfires by distracting the audience from your intended core hashtag. This means you should drop irrelevant, trendy hashtags and instead, try using descriptive hashtags that bring out the core theme of the post you intend to share.

Instagram Basic Features

The characteristics of Instagram as a social platform whose contents are in relation to visuals. Its premises on sharing and viewing graphics, videos, and photos. Its operations and plugins are categorized on its contents: visuals. The idea that it is used only by young people is very wrong. In this section, you will be guided systematically into the features of Instagram for either beginners or professionals. By beginners, it means people that are new to Instagram while professionals mean those familiar or even have an account on the platform. Some of the basic features with their operations include:

The filter options

While uploading pictures on Instagram, the filter is the section which enables you to add enhancements on the photos to be uploaded. These filters make the pictures to look like studio edited ones. They are galvanized with features such as vintage, contrast, light, grayscale, soft glow, and lots more. Try uploading pictures and use this filter to create a special effect on them. Many influencers of Instagram claim that using these filters can make you outstanding among users of Instagram because the sense of filtration is typical only to you. Try it and grow your profile.

Like Button

One of the commonest features on Instagram is the like button. This platform can barely operate without features such as this. This is like an authorization given to fellow users to comment, follow or do anything to your post on the platform. The like button enables users to give either pleasing or unpleasing undertone remark on your posts. With the like button, lots of transformation like increment in the number of followers and the benefits that follow is activated. The like button works in two places: it can be used on the home page, and it can be used as a user's dashboard. When the like button is used at the general page, it only gives remarks on the posts while when it is on the user's dashboard, the person becomes a 'follower.'

The Iconosquare feature

This is a form of a hashtag that is typically used to track campaigns. The performance report of the campaigns is what Iconosquare brings to you. You will be able to see relating data of the hashtag and even the growth alongside engagement of it on the campaign you have created.

The @ feature on Instagram

This is used basically for direct comment. This is for comment on posts on the platform. One could comment by tapping on the comment bubble through the person's username or type @ alongside the username.

The Word Suggestion content

This feature has been designed to help while typing on the platform. With a few words, you will be given any suggestion to make it easier for you to type. In the cases of comment, you will see related words while searching for a username. You will have related usernames.

Instagram set up operations

To download the Instagram app, one needs to consider the iOS of the medium to download it. If you have Android, you will download from 'Google Play.' If you have an iPhone, you will download from the 'App store.' Search these stores, you will, with ease, locate the app.

Registering your Instagram Account

After downloading the Instagram app, you will need to open an account. The app should create a 'shortcut icon' on your homepage after installation: if it didn't check your installed apps. Register your account or log in if you have an account already.

Creating your Instagram Account

Upon the location and clicking on the app, you will need to create a username and password. Your username can be any name combination. At this point your creativity is needed, the username can be a nickname. Care must be taken to use a name familiar to the people in order to facilitate the location and gaining of followers quickly. For example, you might consider using a clip of your first name and surname in uppercase or lowercase as 'TIMSAM' or 'timsam' for Timothy Samuel. After the username, use a password that is familiar with other platforms. You will surely need to add your email account which you could create one for the account. You can choose to add your phone number or not.

Uploading your profile photo

After you have created your account, as part of the process of perfect and strong Instagram account, you will need to add your profile picture. The picture can be taken immediately as you open your account but uploading an existing picture with high quality is highly recommended. Select 'Done' when you have uploaded the picture.

Friends and Family found on Instagram

For capitalization of your account to the full fledge, you will need to follow people that will share your pictures, and you do same to theirs. You can consider giving them your username or search from your account. With increment in followers, there are lots of benefits attached to it.

Adding and Following on Instagram

To be added to an account, you will be on the followers' list. You can follow and be followed respectively. Addition of a user will as well enable you to follow too. However, to randomly add people, you could click on the 'cog icon' on the home screen and click on 'invite friends.' With this, contacts of people around your vicinity will be suggested.

Connect to Social Media

You have an option on the app to search your phonebook directly. Simply click on 'My Contact,' and you will be prompted to search. Contacts with the Instagram account will come up, click on 'Follow' to add them to your account. Then, click on the home icon to return to the home of your account which should show the added accounts.

Home Screen

The icon looks like a house. It will automatically refresh itself when your photo has like, comment or when one of your friends add photos. The home will be updated with data, however.

Profile

The brief story created about you is your profile. The file card at the corner of the home screen contains your profile. Other things at this corner are photos, "following" and "Followers."

Privacy on Instagram

On the 'Edit my Profile' button, you can restrict the people that can view your profile. This is not encouraging, however, for a business person.

Privacy Off/on

When your privacy is turned off, anybody, even outside Instagram, can view your account. When it is switched on, only people following you can view your account.

News Feed

Photos, graphics, and videos are what is contained in the news feed. You can refresh the page by simply swiping it down. The news feeds are selected randomly; you scroll up or down.

Viewing comments from your Friends and family

The photo at the top left of your home screen is used to view people that have commented on your photo. Before clicking on it, there is something in grey color. It is meant to give you information about the comment.

Adding comment

Simply tap the speech bubble at the home screen which will prompt a new page to enable you to write your comment. Send it, and your name will appear right under the comment.

Attached Links

This feature enables people to be prompted to either another user's account or website. It is strategically attached to the account to enhance it. Most likely, it is a business account. If you click on surf new page, you can return to your home by tapping the back button on your phone.

The # Hashtag meaning

This feature is used to publicize a given post. By publicizing it, very many users will have access to the post. When you are using the hashtag, make sure there is no space between it and your post to avoid misunderstanding of your post. Additionally, when a hashtag is added to a post, it appears in blue. There are various reasons Instagram users use the hashtag. Some of these reasons include; promotion of business, gaining more followers, connecting to people that have the same idea and specialization as theirs, etc.

The hashtag enables you to search based on your specific interest on the platform. Your interest varies alongside many other things such as a book, mountain, etc. For instance, you could search with this #mountains. This will give you varying posts relating to your interest. Also, you will see profiles that have the same interest as you. The profiles that will be prompted will be top leading users who will teach you how best to construct your account too.

iOS, Android or Window icon

This particular icon is used to add photos. You can access it by clicking on the blue icon and then the circle at the bottom of the icon. Your gallery will be accessed automatically, and you can add your photo.

Followers icon

This is used to show the people that are following you in numbers. By followers, it simply means those people that your posts, whatsoever, will appear in their news feed. When you click on this icon, you will be able to see pictures of these people and either white color (to show you are following them) or blue button (to show you are yet to follow them).

Star symbols

This is technically referred to as the explore icon. It enables you to access a new page with a square at its top to type your information. With this icon, you can individualize your search. By individualizing, it means that you can search an account by hashtag or nickname. This facilitates a random and quick response from these people when you post. You can as well access their profiles upon searching.

Chapter 9 Twitter Marketing

Twitter is an incredibly powerful tool for influencer marketing, as well as many other marketing techniques. If you are already on Twitter, effectively branding your profile and learning how to leverage influencers on the platform is a wonderful way for you to begin growing into your next level of business. In this chapter, you are going to explore how you can leverage Twitter to grow your business, increase your audience, and reach the next phase of growth for you and your brand. If you are not already on Twitter, using this chapter can help you get started so that you can tap into this tool and grow your business on another great platform.

Branding Your Twitter Profile

Branding your Twitter profile effectively is an important way to make sure that you are creating a profile that is actually going to attract your target audience. When it comes to developing your Twitter reach, a well-developed profile is more clean and complete looking, meaning that people will stop and look at it longer, potentially even following you and engaging with your content. When you are developing your profile, it is important to create with your audience in mind so that they can get a feel for who you are and what you are creating. On Twitter, one study showed that more than 80 percent of people who land on your profile also check out your link, which means that this is a huge conversion you can be tapping into if you leverage your profile effectively.

There are six ways that you can brand your Twitter profile effectively so that your audience gets a complete experience when landing on your profile. These five branding tools are advanced, so whether you are new or mature on the platform, reading through these tips will help you leverage your platform and grow it even stronger.

Fill Out Your Entire Profile

With your brand in mind, make sure that you fill out your entire Twitter profile in a way that clearly reflects your brand. You can do this by ensuring that your username is on brand, your bio is filled out, and you have filled in your website information on your profile. You can also update your profile image with a properly sized branded image, header image, and background image. These three elements allow you to create a graphical aesthetic that is on-brand, making your account even more personalized and enjoyable. You should also place your city or town information in your profile so that people know where your business is located, even if you are a remote business so that you can give people an idea of where you are. Knowing where you are located helps people feel more confident that you are a real person with a location, and that you are not a scammer located overseas trying to get money from people. Essentially, it adds another layer to your online personality.

As you fill everything out, make sure that it all ties together and creates an appealing aesthetic so that your profile is visually enjoyable to spend time on. You want your profile to look attractive so that when people land on it, they are instantly curious to learn more because now you have created visual interest. You can even increase your visual interest by creating custom branding graphics for your page and switching them out every season, ensuring that your page keeps a fresh and attractive feel. Some brands will even adjust their header image every month or every other month as their specials change so that their header behaves like a promotional tool for their brand.

Follow the Right People

On Twitter, following the right people is an imperative tool in helping you generate engagement and get your name out there. When you follow the right people, you develop a group of people that you can engage with, so they begin to see who you are. As they do, they will start to follow you, giving you a following that is going to help you get started as these are the people who will start interacting with your posts as you begin posting them. Early on, really investing in the back and forth engagement process is important to help develop traction with your page, so make sure that you are spending a lot of time following people and then engaging with the people that you are following. As you do, be authentic with your sharing to ensure that you are not coming across as fake or like you are simply trying to use this engagement to grow. Even though that is part of the reason, there should also be the intention that you genuinely want to connect with these people and grow your platform.

Another way that you can use following people as a tool is through recognizing that by following the people in your industry, you are actually turning your feed into market research. When you are following all of the right people, such as people whom you look up to and people who are a part of your target audience, you get to see how your industry is growing and what is trending in your industry. This way, you can begin using the information to develop your content and keep yourself trending in your industry.

Tweet

Before you begin tweeting, there is one very important rule that needs to be made clear: *Twitter is not your electronic billboard.* Your goal when you get on Twitter is not to start blasting your wall with information and assuming that everyone is going to see what you have shared and begin interacting with you. No, Twitter is less about status updates and more about fostering interaction and engagement with your audience. You need to ensure that every update you make is not promoting your company, as this is going to come across as self-serving and spammy. Instead, make every fourth tweet promotional, and all of the others in between about engaging with your audience and starting conversations.

In addition to getting your ratios correct, you also want to make sure that what you are tweeting and how you are tweeting it is relevant to your audience. You want to use keywords that are relevant to your industry so that when people are searching these keywords, your tweets begin coming up. You should also be paying attention to trending keywords in your industry so that you can make use of these, thus increasing your chances of getting found on Twitter. Aside from that, make sure that you are using your personality and personal voice on Twitter so that people can tell you apart from the crowd.

Optimize for Mobile

Twitter is often used on a desktop, but it also has a widely popular mobile app, which means that you need to be thinking about your mobile users as well. In this day and age, there is nothing more frustrating than a business that breaks into the online space and refrains from developing any form of mobile optimization. It makes the business look incomplete and outdated since more and more people are switching to mobile devices as mobile browsers and applications continue to grow in popularity with each passing year.

Fortunately for you, the Twitter app is already optimized for mobile, so there is not much that you need to do to optimize your profile for the mobile app. The primary thing that you need to pay attention to is your graphics—since the graphics may appear differently on a mobile browser. Always take a look to ensure that you are not using an excessively tiny font or images with too intricate of details that are not as easily visible on mobile, as this can make it your profile frustrating to browse on mobile. Always make sure that anytime you update your images, you peek at what they look like on a mobile setting so that you are confident that what your audience is seeing is professional and easy to see.

Integrate Twitter Elsewhere

Lastly, a well-branded and well-established Twitter account should be integrated elsewhere beyond Twitter itself. Make sure to add follow buttons on your website, in your emails, and anywhere else that Twitter follow buttons can be added so that anytime someone comes across you online, they find your Twitter, too. If you run a blog, one particularly powerful integration is to use a plugin that allows you to feature relevant tweets in your blog posts so that people who are on Twitter can retweet your relevant tweets. This way, not only can they retweet you and get you in front of their audience, but they can also follow you and begin consuming even more of your content through Twitter, making it a win-win situation!

The Importance of Your Personality

When it comes to branding yourself anywhere online, making your personality clearly visible to the outside world is imperative. There is nothing worse than coming across a well-designed and well-positioned brand only to find that it lacks any true originality, making it sound just like every other brand that is attempting to grow in the online space. Getting your personality into your message and being authentic is an important part of really getting your message out there and growing as a personal brand.

This message applies not only for Twitter but for all personal branding strategies: if you are too afraid to speak up and be yourself, you are going to have a hard time getting heard by anyone who cares. The internet is filled with people who are afraid to be original because they are afraid to be rejected or disliked by the people around them. It can be scary to think about what might happen if you put yourself out there in a personal way and later find that you are not well received, on many levels. Even so, getting past this fear and putting yourself out there as far as your branding is concerned is necessary if you are going to get heard and develop yourself as a personal brand. You need to be willing to share your originality and show people the authentic side of you that makes you different from the crowd.

On Twitter specifically, do not be afraid to tweet with humor and share your real thoughts in relation to everything going on in the world. Talk about what you think, share your real opinions, and do not be afraid to be the real you. The more you share your authentic personality, the more people who are looking for someone just like you are going to find you and start paying attention to what you are saying. As a result, you will find yourself feeling a lot more received by your audience because they can actually find you.

As you continue sharing in this more authentic way, you will also begin to discover what types of conversations your audience enjoys having so that you know what to talk to them about. This way, you can start plenty of rich conversations through your posts, which goes a long way in terms of developing relationships with your audience. As people continue responding and developing these relationships with you, they will also continue to pay more attention to your sales posts, and will likely be more interested in paying attention to what it is that you are selling. Now, rather than just being another person promoting to them on Twitter, you are a genuine personality who is offering them a product or a service that they are interested in. You have taken the time to get to know them and develop a relationship with them, so now they trust when you say you have something that they may be interested in because they trust that you know them enough to know whether or not they actually would be.

As you can see, truly taking the time to invest in relationships online, especially on a social platform like Twitter, which thrives on conversation, you are doing your business and growth a massive favor. You want to continue emphasizing these conversations and relationships, and trust that through them, your business will grow massively and effectively.

Maximizing Growth

Once you get on Twitter, you must begin focusing on how you can maximize your growth quickly. The sooner you can develop a healthy following, the sooner you are going to be able to convert through Twitter as you will have a large enough audience to market to. Growing on Twitter is similar to growing on other platforms, although there are some strategies you can take into consideration to help you get your name out there more consistently, thus making it easier for people to find you. The thing that you need to remember about Twitter is that you need to make a big "splash" actually to get seen and followed by people. People follow those on Twitter who know how to be the life of the party, who can spark a conversation or jump in on a conversation and make it livelier, and who possess a high amount of charisma. If you want to excel on Twitter, you need to be prepared to become a loud expression of yourself so that you can be heard amongst the sea of other people who are also participating in conversations on Twitter. This is how you can go from being present to being present *and known.*

Because of how Twitter works—having a limited number of characters to use for updates and conversations—, you need to be ready to be upfront about what you are sharing from the get-go. In other words, do not waste your time burying the lead as this will result in you having your audience ignore you since they cannot get to the bottom of what you are trying to say. Be blunt, to the point, and very clear in what you are saying in every single post so that people always know what you are saying and what you mean.

Another thing you need to consider when it comes to growing on Twitter is that people are only going to see so many of the recent tweets on their pages—they are not on the platform all day every day scrolling to see what you and everyone else is saying. As a result, you can benefit from reiterating the same tweet in a few different ways to ensure that your entire audience sees what you have posted and gets the value out of the tweet that you have shared.

Make sure that you think before you tweet, as well. When it comes to thinking before you tweet, doing so can prevent you from sharing anything that may come across as derogatory or rude. For example, a company known as DiGiorno's pizza used a hashtag known for raising awareness around domestic violence to promote their pizza deals that week. They later had to issue a professional apology statement, as this came across as demeaning and rude to the people who were actually using the hashtag to promote something positive. Not all press is good press, especially in a generation of people who are becoming more and more consciously aware of how language and behaviors affect the people around them. Thinking critically about how your tweet will be received before making it is also especially important for smaller brands or personal brands who may not have as large of a following as existing corporations. For you, every follower counts, so you need to be mindful and respectful of your followers when you are generating posts.

Lastly, always give credit where credit is due as it does not come across as authentic or genuine to share someone else's content and appear as though you are attempting to pass it off as your own. Tagging the original content creator, using the acronym "RT" which stands for "retweet" or using the words "via" before sharing who originally shared the content can all help you give credit to the original content creator. Online, everyone is trying to make a living or get their name out there, so you have to be sure that you are being respectful to the other people who are also trying to generate success online. Furthermore, nothing will tank your success faster than making it appear as though you are attempting to take ownership of someone else's work. If you get caught plagiarizing content, you *will* be penalized for it, and likely very harshly. A great example of this is Audrey Kitching, who has a massive online following, and an equally massive number of people resisting her because they have found that she regularly steals content. Whether or not she actually does is unimportant; the fact is that she has become well known for this behavior and, as a result, has stunted her growth in a big way. If you stay authentic and always give credit where credit is due, then you can keep your reputation clean and your audience happy. Integrity is key.

Finding Influencers on Twitter

Twitter is another great platform for discovering influencers on, and leveraging influencers on Twitter is an equally excellent way to get your brand out there even further. Finding influencers on Twitter is similar to finding them elsewhere—you begin searching for content that is relevant to your industry, and then you start searching for the individuals who are making the biggest impact on Twitter through their posts. The key here is to know what you are looking for so that as you vet your Twitter influencers, you can be confident that you are getting the best ones. Unlike on Instagram or Facebook, vetting Twitter influencers is done in a slightly different way.

When you are looking for an influencer on Twitter, start by getting clear on the type of influencer that you are looking for. Ideally, you should be writing down what it is that they share, how they connect with your target audience, and what their personality is like. You want to find influencers who are sharing content that is relevant to what you offer, who connect with your target audience in a way that makes them likely to make sales, and who has a personality that will be a positive reflection for your brand. Finding the right influencer who is going to compliment your brand effectively is important to ensure that any money you invest into this influencer deal is going to be well spent, and you are going to get positive gains out of it.

Once you have identified who it is that you are looking for, you can begin finding influencers in your field who match these characteristics. Make sure that you are looking for people who fit these three categories first, as these need to be your priorities in whom you are searching for. You can pay attention to follower count and engagement content after— when you have identified a few people who already fit your needs as a brand.

When you are ready to begin looking at the influencer's metrics, you want to pay attention to engagement ratio more than anything else. On Twitter, a large following does not necessarily equal a large impact, so you need to be careful to ensure that the person you intend to work with does actually receive a high engagement ratio. The better their engagement ratio, the higher your chances of getting conversions through that influencer. Of course, this does come with a certain condition. If you have found someone who has incredible engagement ratios yet they are only getting engagement from tens of people or maybe a few hundred people, you are likely looking at someone who is not going to be able to create the impact that you need or desire. You want someone who has a high engagement ratio that earns them several hundred or even several thousand engagements per post, to ensure that they are someone who will make an impact. Once you have secured that fact, you can begin making content with your potential influencers so that you can start making deals with them. At this point, everything you do is going to be the same as you would have done on any other social media platform. You will still want to conduct yourself professionally, create legal documents outlining your deals, and be cooperative so that the influencer enjoys working with you and is likely to boost your reputation rather than minimize it due to your own misrepresentation of your brand.

Chapter 10 YouTube Marketing

To start working with YouTube, you have to use several steps to help you get on the site and to produce videos. Fortunately, you can get everything ready easily.

Create a Profile

Get your own profile on YouTube ready at the start. To use You Tube you need to log into Google Plus. This is the system that Google uses to give access to various online services and to be listed on Google. It is typically a good idea for a business to register with Google and Google Plus just to add your contact information and other details, but also to use YouTube for marketing.

To get your profile set, do the following:

1. Register for a Google Plus profile.

You will have to go to the Google website and click on the Sign in button to create an account. Enter a user name, a password, and your current email address and other details. You will have to verify your account with a text to a mobile number. Then you can get onto YouTube to create your own channel.

The best thing to do is to get a brand account ready. A brand account is like a personal Google Plus profile but for businesses instead. You should upload your videos through your brand account so people can see what you have to offer. Refer to the Google Plus section of this book to see how to get a brand account set up.

As you get on YouTube, open the My Channel link on the left-hand side of the screen.

2. Click on the option to use a business or other name for your channel.

3. Enter the brand account name you wish to use.

Click on the About page.

4. Click the proper edit button on the page to enter details on what your site offers.

Be direct when telling people about the products and services you offer. Imitate the following points:

- Add keywords onto your page. This makes it easier to spot your work when a search is conducted. Make sure the keywords relate to what you are promoting.

- Explain who will post on the site and how often you might add things onto the page.

- Insert a few additional links. You can add links to other social media sites or your personal website.

7. Add a personal profile photo. Click on the small box on the top-left part of the screen to add an avatar photo. This is where people will see when you post things onto other pages.

Depending on what you entered into Google Plus, you might already have a profile photo listed. You can always change the photo if desired.

8. Add a header for your channel. Go to the top-right corner to open an option for changing the image you will display on that header. This is entered next to the avatar photo.

Go to the gear icon near the top-right part of the screen where the subscribe button is. Click and then choose to customize the layout of your channel.

Your channel page can be laid out in any way you want. Choose to add specific videos that you want to show first on a page. Additionally, sort between the view subscribers will see and what non-subscribers will notice. This lets you promote your work to others in a better light.

Get the Proper Equipment For Your Video

You could technically use a camera on a Smartphone or tablet to produce videos promoting your business on YouTube. That does not mean working with something rudimentary is a good option. The problem with such a small camera is that it will not pick up audio well. It won't produce a great picture either. You should use something a little more professional for the best results.

To get a video recorded:

1. Get a proper camera that can record well. A small high-definition camera is useful.

GoPro cameras are especially popular. Such cameras are becoming increasingly more affordable. Make sure that you know how to operate it.

Pay attention to the microphone feature on the camera. A camera needs to have a good microphone although a separate attachment might be needed if you have a smaller unit. Try to keep the microphone off-screen.

2. Look at the lighting you are using. Review how everything photographs so you can get a proper layout that looks great.

3. Look at the benefits of a video editing tool. Use it to produce a variety of special effects or overlays on your video.

You can employ various video editing programs for your YouTube video. Pinnacle Studio, Virtual Dub, and iMovie are among the top options. You could still edit features on your video directly through YouTube although it might be easier to take advantage of something more professional.

Uploading the Video

The process for recording and editing your video is clearly up to you. Next, pay attention to how you your video will be added onto YouTube.

To upload a video onto YouTube:

1. Click the download icon on the top-right part of the screen.

Select a video from your hard drive.

2. Enter the title and description.

The title should include a listing of what your video is about. It could include a keyword relating to the video's content.

The description is where you will add the detailed information on the video. It is also where you can place your business URL and other links.

4. Enter a series of tags.

The tags describe what is in the video. They can appear when someone is searching for your video. Use as many tags as you have to, but try to be specific. Refer to what you talk about in the video and location.

Click the social media links or other features that you use to share the video.

You can share your video on other sites by clicking the proper icons on the right-hand side of the upload screen. Share it on Facebook, Twitter, or other sites connected to your profile. You can also add a message through the platform to let people know to watch your video. (Don't forget that people who watch your video can use the YouTube player to forward a video to another social media site too.)

6. Select the thumbnail you want to use.

You can always choose a random slide from your video as a thumbnail that people will see before watching your video. You can also have your own custom thumbnail that you can upload.

7. Click on the Advanced Settings section to make some adjustments.

Enter many things on the Advanced Setting section to improve how your video works. Your video can allow the following features:

- The ability to post comments.

- The option to only display comments you approve.

- Allow users to leave ratings for your video.

- Distribution settings including the option to embed a video or to publish on a subscriber's page.

- Enable age restriction; this means that you will keep underage viewers from watching your videos although you cannot promote the video in an ad campaign.

- Select the category for your video; these include entertainment, how-to, and news categories.

8. Click the Publish button at the top-right corner of the screen to get the video uploaded. It should be fully accessible to all.

Editing Your Video Through YouTube

Although a video editor can help you before you upload your video to YouTube, there might be times when you have to edit a video after it is online. This is due to YouTube's system possibly affecting the general quality of the video. Maybe you might even find an issue that you want to resolve, but you never noticed it until after you uploaded your video. Fortunately, YouTube does have its own feature to edit videos. Use this feature if you need extra help to make the video more attractive.

To edit your videos:

1. Go to the Creator Studio on your YouTube channel.

Click on the Edit button on the specific video that you want to edit.

Click the small arrow next to the button to choose what you want to edit. This takes you directly to one of the features.

3. Use the Info and Settings tab to edit the description, tags, and other features.

4. Use the Enhancements section to add light, contrast, etc.

Click on the Trim button on the Enhancements section to cut any parts of a video if necessary. This might work if you want to eliminate excess material that might not be professional or attractive.

You can do many other special things within the Edit menu under the Creator Studio section.

Adding Music

You can add background music to your YouTube video. This is great if you need some music in the background. It works better than having a plain video with silence in the background. Here's how to add music:

1. Go to the Music panel on the Edit menu of the Creator Studio.
2. Search for a track to use. You can choose something based on what is popular or on a certain genre.
3. Click any of the music files to find what you feel comfortable with.
4. Select the confirm button on the menu when finished.

YouTube has tens of thousands of music files you can use for the background of your video. These are all ad-free options to use without having to pay anything extra.

You can always use your own music to add onto your video before you upload it. That would require the use of a professional program. You would have to be aware of how the music is made and who owns the rights as you don't want to violate any copyright terms on YouTube.

Fortunately, the music files that YouTube does offer are diverse and come in many forms. They are certified by YouTube to be free for use. You will not run into any legal problems featuring these music files.

Adding an End Screen

The next thing to decide on is an end screen. This feature of YouTube appears during the final few seconds of a video. It lets you highlight other videos you want to direct people toward. Use this to get people to see other videos relating to something your business offers. Only choose appropriate videos that are relevant to the original one. This is so people see something related to their interests. Your content also has to be compelling enough for someone to click one of the videos you are promoting.

You can insert many things onto your end screen. You can add some thumbnails that link up to other videos on your YouTube channel, a link to a website, or a call-to-action to get people to subscribe to your channel.

To prepare the right end screen features:

1. Go to the End Screen section of the Video Creator Studio editor on the video of your choosing.
2. Your video must be at least 25 seconds in length to be able to add an end screen.
3. Go to the proper section of the video where you want to add an end screen.
   You can only add the end screen during the final 20 seconds of your video.
4. Click the Add Element option.
5. Select the specific item you want to add.

You can add a link to a website provided you have one that has been properly approved. You could also add a link to promote subscriptions to your channel or a link to another video or playlist.

Drag the individual items that you have added as desired.

You can move them around various parts of the screen. But watch what is on your video at the end, so you don't add these things in the wrong spots.

The end screen is great for marketing as it draws in more subscribers and lets people know that you have more to share. Use this if you have a lot of videos you want to show or you simply want to obtain some extra subscribers. Whatever your goal, you will find it easy for you to get people to your spot when the end screen is created properly.

Can You Add Annotations?

There is an Annotations listing on the Creator Studio menu, but it is not something you can use. Annotations were offered by YouTube, but they are no longer included as they cannot be read on mobile devices. Many people on YouTube preferred to disable annotations on their videos.

These features were boxes that could be added onto a video. These boxes included additional bits of information relating to something being posted. Anyone could use an annotation to add notes about what is on the screen. Fortunately, a person can easily use the end screen feature to give the same messages.

Do not be surprised if you notice annotations on older videos when comparing what your competitors might be using. Existing annotations on videos that were created before YouTube did away with them will still appear. However, they can no longer be edited.

If anything, the end screen is more convenient. It is not intrusive and distraction- free. It also offers better space for things to say and actual links that might be more valuable.

Add Cards

Adding cards allows you to ask people to send feedback about your videos among other things. A card is something that appears at any point in a video and invites people to interact. Here are some steps for producing such a card:

1. Go to the Creator Studio and then to the Card section on the space you want to edit.
2. Select Add Card from one of various cards.
   You can add a poll, a card promoting your channel, a donation card for nonprofit fundraising, or a link card that goes to your website. Any of these can work if the content you have is valuable and useful.
3. Enter the details. These include a link you want people to visit, a donation button, or a poll. The screen will produce a proper interface for any of these.
4. Choose where you want to place the card. You will have a bit of freedom as to where the card can go.

Getting your videos on YouTube up and running is easy to do when the right plans are made. YouTube has laid out everything you need right through its website. You can use all the resources YouTube provides to help you make the most in marketing your business. Best of all, much of what is offered is free to use. All you need now is a camera to record your videos. You could use editing tools on your own as well, but that's another story.

Chapter 11 Flickr

Photo sharing has transformed into an incredibly noticeable approach to manage showcase things and organizations on the web.

Flickr is one of the channels that made an impact on cutting edge exhibiting and its acclaim spread like crazy flame. It is an online photo sharing task that empowers you to incorporate your things in an interfacing way and even offers the most profitable results for your business when fused to your web based life the board structure.

Using Flickr for Digital Marketing

There's nothing more required than a few minutes to set up your record on Flickr and join distinctive people by exchanging and sharing your photos. Flickr's free record allows up to 100MB exchange each month and there is a probability for you to refresh if the free accumulating it gives isn't sufficient to you.

To empower you to take in progressively about Flickr, here is a smart look on the preferences that it can bring especially for the people who promote their things and organizations on the web.

The Benefits of Having a Flickr Account:

Huge Storage:

Flickr offers 100MB of free storing each month with the exception of you can climb to a PRO record if 100MB isn't adequate to work your necessities. With Flickr, you can exchange pictures for a similar number of as you need!

Versatility:

Flickr is a photo sharing site that engages you to make the best of your innovativeness. Next to empowering you to exchange photos, it has features that license changing of photo names, titles, and even generation of photo sets.

Never-ending Back-up:

Flickr offers the protection that you requirement for your significant photos since it surrenders an interminable back to ensure that photos will be available and guaranteed to serve your necessities.

Visitor Friendly:

Flickr isn't just for record holders since it consolidates features that empower visitors to comment on photos, incorporate notes, and watch photo slideshows. Visitors can even purchase in to RSS channel so they can see the latest pictures that you exchanged.

Extraordinary Functionality:

Flickr has a component that grants resaving and resizing of pictures. It is similarly simple to utilize so making your photos perceivable is a direct technique.

Blogging Compatibility:

Flickr also extends its degree to bloggers. Blogging is a champion among the most supported ways to deal with offer news and information. By using Flickr it will be less requesting to bestow pictures to your blog disciples.

Openness of untouchable Tools:

Flickr can be utilized using untouchable mechanical assemblies. By using free online life the administrators programming like Postific, you can without quite a bit of a stretch work with your photographs and make the best of your progressed exhibiting exertion.

Consider Upgrading to Flickr Pro

Like other web-based life accounts, Flickr offers the option for record customers to climb to an ace record that offers increasingly important favorable circumstances. Expecting almost no exertion, account holders will have the ability to get Flickr Pro and value these extra favorable circumstances:

Unlimited Storage:

Flickr Pro allows usage of limitless extra space, and that infers you can exchange photos that can outperform up to 1TB.

Photo Statistics:

By refreshing your record to Flickr Pro, you will have the ability to checks and referrer bits of knowledge for your photos. This is one of the features that a huge amount of specialists regard since it exhibits where a photo has been used or associated over the general web.

Photo Replacement:

With a Flickr Pro record, customers can replace photos without having to reupload them. They can even archive high-objectives exceptional pictures and welcome a commercial free difficulty while using their records.

Higher Upload Limit:

Flickr Pro not just offers vast limit and exchange speed, since record holders can in like manner misuse new exchange limits. Using a Flickr Pro record, photo exchanges should be conceivable with up to 200MB in size and 1GB per video.

Flickr is a champion among the most settled players and can end up a standout amongst your most dependable web-based systems administration displaying devices. Not in any way like other photo sharing goals, Flickr offers photo sharing social events. It has been used for photo sharing for a long time starting at now and remains to be the favored choice of real picture takers.

In case you are into cutting edge advancing and characteristics the power of pictures, Flickr is a decision that you can't stand to reject. Use it with an electronic life the board gadget for business and undoubtedly, you will have the ability to develop brand care no problem!

Chapter 12 Tumblr

Tumblr is a fabulous stage to achieve a large number of potential clients. When choosing whether Tumblr is directly for your web-based life advertising efforts, you generally need to figure, by what method will it advantage your clients. In this part, I will breakdown what Tumblr is, and how you can utilize it further bolstering your good fortune.

What Type of Platform is Tumblr?

Tumblr is a cross breed blog arrange and casual association. Customers can post media content (photos, delineations, chronicles, music, GIFS, etc.) to a blog, seek after each other and comment on each other's posts. (You do have the decision to make your blog private.)

Who Utilizes It?

Customer numbers are hard to tie, yet work it to express that numerous people use Tumblr – which stunned me! Dependent upon the source, Tumblr has 300 million or barely short of 500 million web diaries, web journals and 400 million or 600 multi month to month customers.

Most customers are around the world – only 65% of development begins from the US. Customers are in like manner energetic – youths and Millennials. So it ought not stun anybody that a bigger piece of customers visit the site from their phones. Thus, in case you are attempting to contact people some place in the scope of 13 and 30 years old far and wide, genuinely, use Tumblr.

How Does Tumblr contrast from Facebook and different stages

The gigantic focus on Tumblr is quality over sum. Building critical associations and teaming up with various customers is unquestionably more fundamental than having a zillion aficionados or fans. So in the event that you will use it for advancing, you should concentrate on successfully enamoring with different people.

In like manner realize that it's stacked up with claim to fame systems and subcultures, immense quantities of whom have their own one of a kind eccentric lingo.

The most effective method to utilize Tumblr for Marketing Your Business

Pick a Catchy Name

Tumblr web diaries will when all is said in done have smart, sly or critical names, as Tor VPN Bear. Everything considered, there's nothing out of order with using your picture name. Additionally, it'll help with brand affirmation.

Get Creative

All around advancing messages on Tumblr won't go over well. You ought to be inconspicuous. Discharge your creative side and post content that is useful, hopeful and happy.

Continuously Provide Links to Your Site

For sure, it is OK to offer associates with your site, especially in the event that you're running an unprecedented progression. Basically, ensure those presents are more close on home than what you may continue running on Facebook or Instagram.

Try to Pay Attention to Customers Wants and Needs

The better you know your social event of individuals, the better your substance will do on Tumblr – just like some other stage. What questions do your social event of individuals have? What information do they strive after? That is what you need to post on Tumblr.

Utilize Tags

Marks and labels are comparably as basic on Tumblr as hashtags are on Instagram – they'll empower your substance to get found in interest. 10 to 15 labels for each post is flawless, just guarantee they're look terms that people are using.

Become dynamic

Since quality collaboration is so basic, the more you put in, the more you'll get out. Seek after various locales and leave comments. This will raise your detectable quality and help you pull in supporters.

Chapter 13 Goodreads

Goodreads is an incredible informal community where millions interface by means of their writer page, yet it isn't just for writers, we can utilize this site for web based life promoting purposes too.

How has Goodreads turned out to be so broad? All things considered, similar to Amazon, individuals can locate their preferred books and see fair audits. It resembles an extraordinary enormous virtual Facebook, Barnes and Noble store with Amazon folded into one.

When you open a peruser account on Goodreads, you fundamentally can tell different adherents what books you like, what books you are right now perusing and even make gatherings and subjects identified with your preferences, post surveys and the sky is the limit from there!

To get to know Goodreads you should simply agree to accept a record at www.goodreads.com and after that start investigating. The site will walk you through the methods for utilizing it, Goodreads is very easy to use. There is no cost to joining, and is a huge amount of fun!

So have you joined? Stunning. Here are some ways you can Goodreads for advancing your business.

1. Setup an Author Page

Time: 1-2 hours

Getting an essayist page is the underlying advance to connect with your perusers on Goodreads. Consider this your Facebook page anyway on Goodreads. Making an author page will give you experiences about your books and will give your perusers a spot to see what you are up to and what you are scrutinizing.

You can find how to join the Goodreads Author program. This page has point by point headings that will walk you very much arranged through the setup strategy.

2. Solicitation that Your Readers List Your Books on Listopia

Time: 30 minutes

The Listopia portion of Goodreads has a summary for each kind of book conceivable. Guarantee your books are on the best possible records.

You can find this portion at:

http://www.goodreads.com/list

Every now and again the differentiation some place in the scope of 30th and tenth on these once-overs is only two or three votes. So the more your perusers vote the higher your books will rank.

3. Advance

Time: 1 hour + $20

This is optional anyway worth the effort. Goodreads has a pivotal book-advancing system that empowers you to target people who have very assessed unequivocal scholars. Are your books like James Scott Bell? You can concentrate on his fans with an ad for your book.

You can in like manner use this instrument to target people who have assessed your books previously. You may have fans who loved your diverse books and who have no idea about your latest book. Goodreads empowers you to connect with those perusers.

The advancements can cost as small as $0.15 per click. This is a standout amongst the most affordable ways to deal with enlighten your perusers concerning your new book.

4. Do Book Giveaways

Time: 1 hour + books + shipping

All things considered; 850 people enter each Goodreads book giveaway. Of the people who enter, they will add the book to their to-examine rundown and half of the victors will complete a survey for the book. Goodreads has a book giveaways region arranged unequivocally to empower you to expose issues about your books.

5. Setup Groups and Discuss Books

Time: 1 Hour

Goodreads empowers you to have a book exchange about your book. This empowers your perusers to make request and talk with each other about your book. This is an unprecedented technique to change lukewarm perusers into eager book evangelists. You can be as connected with these book trades as you should be. The key is to start the discourse and after that let your perusers take it starting there. For the methods on the most capable strategy to start a book trade, visit Goodread's Featured Books.

6. Interface Your Blog to Goodreads

Time: 20 minutes

Did you understand that Goodreads will email your fans once per multi day stretch of all your new blog sections? This is a phenomenal strategy to help perusers for you blog for all intents and purposes zero work. Basically, set it up once and subsequently you don't need to worry over it. Blog blend is one of the preferences you get when you join the Goodreads Author Program.

7. Approach fans for legit Reviews

Time: 30 minutes

GoodReads features books reliant on the amount of studies. Try not to fear negative audits. The most basic thing these days is the amount of reviews. The more audits your book has the more popular it looks. The more noticeable it looks the more people read it.

Begin utilizing Goodreads today! This site is best stayed quiet diamond in web based life promoting

Chapter 14 The Best Way to Approach Social Media Marketing

Sometimes, even when you follow all the necessary steps, you may not get as many online engagements as you desire. So, here are a few tips and tricks to drive online traffic.

Use hashtags

Hashtags are basically tag to help find things of a similar nature in one place. This is precisely why you should always use hashtags with your promotion, since it will help your post reach beyond your network to people searching for similar items or services. This is especially useful when using Twitter or Instagram to promote your brand.

Email marketing

Email marketing is often one of the most overlooked methods of driving online traffic, but this should not be the case, especially since technology has allowed over 3.8 billion people to use email. Moreover, people now use email apps that have their own custom notification sounds, making it quite impossible to avoid noticing when emails are received.

Analytics
Free-to-use analytics like Google Analytics are a great way to increase online traffic. If used properly and regularly, these can accurately show you which strategies and types of content work the best, in turn, giving you an idea of what to improve and what to let go of.

Backlinks
Backlinks are links to your website or products from another website. These are great to use to drive online traffic. Backlinks enable your website to be exposed to a bigger

audience than your own network. Moreover, trust from Google increases on your backlink with the more trusted websites that point to it, leading to a higher ranking and more exposure and traffic.

Google search advertising

Although this is a paid option, it can be a great one to use for driving traffic to your website. The way this works is that you will have to pay Google a certain amount of money for your website to be included in the top search results for certain keywords.

Stay updated

The best way to drive traffic is to stay updated with what is happening in the social media world. You should always find out which hot topic everyone is talking about, and then you can use this information to your advantage by tying your products or services to that topic. Not only does this drive more traffic, it also creates a positive image of your brand in the minds of people who view your posts.

Conclusion

The world of Social Media is a constantly evolving one. Competition is good though because it brings about disruptive innovation. That's why each social media platform is constantly enhancing and introducing new features to stay relevant to its audiences, giving them better tools to share their content, better ways to engage, and more interesting ways to publish content.

One of the best ways to engage in social media marketing for your business is first to use it as a personal platform for personal use. Use it as an experiment, play around with it, upload images, and get used to it before you embark on opening up an account for your business. This way, you'll be better equipped to make a decision whether that particular social media is worth your time and effort or not and you will also know how audiences in different platforms react to content.

Social Media Marketing, on the other hand, has many benefits, and it does a lot to improve site traffic and help a business reach more customers. Not only that, social media marketing helps brands have a better understanding of their audience and learning from them- their purchasing habits, their likes, dislikes, interests, and so on.

Any business stands a chance to lose out on its customer base if they do not evolve with current times. That said no business would lose out by investing in social media.

SOCIAL MEDIA MARKETING FOR BEGINNERS

SOCIAL MEDIA MARKETING FOR BEGINNERS: A STEP-BY-STEP BEGINNERS GUIDE TO FACEBOOK, INSTAGRAM, LINKEDIN MARKETING - DISCOVER NEW ONLINE TRENDS TO SHAPE THE PERFECT STRATEGY FOR MANAGING YOUR BUSINESS.

Description

The whole world looks to be caught during a compulsive social media craze. Everyone is talking concerning using social media platforms for participating their audience, increasing believability, and building solid brands. There's a marked shift from selling to building relationships, which the social media sites do remarkably well. By definition, social media marketing is nothing however a technique of gaining traffic or audience attention for your business through the utilization of social media. The strategy usually involves concentrating marketing efforts on creating highly engaging content that attracts the attention of your target audience, and encourages them to share it throughout their virtual networks.

Unlike traditional marketing channels, social media marketing doesn't focus on hard selling (though there can be exceptions based on the nature of your business). It is about leveraging the power of audience relationships and forging strong connections through engagement. Social media marketing is concerning constantly growing your audience base by making perceptive and compelling content. It helps marketers build dramatic brands, fosters client loyalty, and lays the inspiration for marketing.

Think of your social media selling as exciting toppings on the dish of your selling combine. They add a lot of punch and panache to your selling efforts. Social media marketing makes your marketing techniques a lot of fascinating, creative, and appealing to your target audience. It adds aa lot of personal character to your robotic selling efforts.

Let's take a real-life example to establish how social media marketing works. You walk into a department store to buy lipstick or perfume. The salesperson at the counter quickly tries to understand what you want and launches into a tiresome and monotonous script about how XYZ is the bestselling fragrance or lipstick currently. You get frustrated with the whole thing because they are showing you everything that you don't want. The salesperson is not actually helping you buy, but rather trying to sell what they think you should buy. They haven't listened to you or tried to tune in to your requirements. Finally, you move to another store.

This guide will focus on the following:

- The Fundamentals of Social Media Marketing
- Why my business needs social media?
- Defining your audience
- Using social media platforms for marketing
- Social media strategy
- The Personal Reality of Personal Branding
- Be professional
- Facebook Marketing
- Instagram Marketing
- YouTube Marketing
- LinkedIn
- Snapchat Marketing
- Success Tips
- Mistakes to Avoid... AND MORE!!!

Dive in, and enjoy the process!

Introduction

Social media has traversed far greater heights than simply being a medium for user-generated content. Today, it's a tool for consumer empowerment (we all witness big conglomerates being brought to their knees by that one dissatisfied tweet or widely shared post) and a gratifying brand-consumer partnership.

Even companies that have long been dismissing social media as frivolous and flippant have started taking note of its benefits. They've realized that social media is not limited to games and light-hearted opinion polls (which are also hugely successful in creating affable brands), but can involve more serious discussions and insights that are invaluable when it comes to building strong brands.

One of the best things about social media is that it is amazingly varied and versatile. Some platforms like Pinterest and Instagram are invaluable tools for visually inclined businesses like home décor, cooking, and graphic artists. Meanwhile, channels like LinkedIn and Google+ are ideal for corporate buzz sharing. Twitter and Facebook are flexible enough to be used by businesses of almost all types. With some ingenuity and resourcefulness, even small businesses can create a storm over social media.

Unlike traditional marketing mediums, social media doesn't swallow a huge chunk of your advertising and promotion budget. You don't need to create cost-intensive and ineffectual marketing plans that leave you broke.

All you need is some creativity, perceptiveness, and an intuitive understanding about your audience's needs. More than sharp business acumen, you need a human touch.

Social media gives your brand a human angle without breaking the bank.

Have you seen any of the Whole Foods videos posted on their corporate Facebook page? They frequently post how-to videos in a subject that their customers are primarily interested in – cooking. The short videos, running for about 40-60 seconds, cover multiple elements such as animation, images, and text. At the end of the video, there is an item for sale that customers can buy to prepare the recipe mentioned in the video.

One such inventive video demonstrated how customers could transform leftover Thanksgiving turkey into—hold your breath—nachos. What a refreshing change from the same old boring sandwiches! It isn't surprising that these videos are hugely popular and the products mentioned at the end are quickly grabbed up by eager viewers. They must be doing something right!

Rather than using long-winded sales pitches to glorify their products, Whole Foods is adding value to their followers' lives by sharing insanely creative ideas and making life more convenient for them. The company is showing customers ways through which their products can actually benefit them. Ingenious? Yes. Simple? Doubly yes.

Though it seems overwhelmingly complex for a beginner, especially given all the information available over the Internet, social media marketing can be relatively simple and effective.

You really do not have to be a marketing expert to master social media. All you need is some inventiveness, unwavering enthusiasm to keep learning new trends, and an empathetic touch to understand your audience.

Chapter 1 The Fundamentals of Social Media Marketing

This book will be covering methods of optimizing four platforms: Facebook, YouTube, Instagram and Pinterest. Each platform will receive its own section, where we will cover all of the tips and tricks to make the most out of each one. However, before we get to the specifics, there are quite a few fundamentals of Social Media Marketing that should be learned and understood before moving into specialization.

This section is dedicated to helping you, the reader, learn how to properly utilize Social Media for the purpose of marketing in all ways. These principles are universal, meaning that regardless of the platform that you use, they are still applicable.

Fundamental One: The Relationship Dynamic

The core of social media marketing is forming relationships with others. Social media itself is a tremendous tool for connection, an innovation that allows for unparalleled access to each other's lives. People engage with social media for a wide variety of reasons, but all of those reasons can be boiled down to one concept: they are looking for connection.

Social media allows us to connect in ways that were unthinkable in previous centuries. The ability to share information at the speed of a button click, the ability to send messages to friends halfway across the world, all of these things are meant to bring people closer together. And for the most part, social media has been wildly successful in connecting us to one another.

When people get on social media, they are looking for different experiences. Some are looking for interesting and engaging content, others are looking for things that make them laugh, but at the core, everyone is searching for something that connects to them on a deeper level. Even if they can't quite verbalize it, the truth is that people use social media as a means to find something greater than themselves.

It can be easy to approach social media marketing with a callous, removed thought process. Rather than looking at these platforms as ways of connection, we can often make the mistake of looking at them as ways of simply making money. This transactionary approach to social media isn't only ineffective, it's also extremely limiting to your potential as a business. Why? Because if we only look at social media as a means to generate revenue, we are denying the opportunity to form relationships with our customers.

Remember, people use social media because they are looking for some kind of connection. They are looking to form relationships. This might not be readily apparent from the outside, but the fact is that the most basic human need is a need to belong, the need to feel as if they are a part of something.

As a social media marketer, you don't just want sales. Sales are wonderful and vital to your business, but they aren't the only goal. Rather, the end goal of social media marketing is to create strong enough relationships with your customers that they become followers of your company and your brand. In other words, they become members of your tribe.

A tribe member isn't simply a customer, but rather they become an advocate of your product or business. They speak on your behalf. They share your content. When others ask for recommendations, they are quick to share a link to your website. They become ardent followers of your company and continue to buy your products with each release.

No doubt, a tribe member is significantly more important than a simple sale. A sale is a transaction, a tribe member is for life. The question is, how can we get people to follow our tribe? And the answer to that question is, of course, social media.

Social media allows for us to form relationships with our customers in ways that were unheard of even 15 years ago. We can answer questions directly; we can share sneak previews to those who follow our groups and we can show the heart and pulse of our brand in ways that catch the interest and attention of our followers. More importantly, we can listen to what our followers have to say. We can take heed to their words, engage in a dialogue and work with them to create a better future for our company.

For social media marketing efforts to be truly successful, it is necessary to walk the line between advertising and engaging. Of course, you want to advertise your products, get them to visit your links and generate sales, but you cannot neglect the social aspect. If you work on forming relationships first, the sales will come rolling in. However, if you neglect building relationships with your customers and only focus on promoting your products, you may get sales, but you certainly won't get tribe members.

So how can we form these relationships? How can we create these bonds that turn a customer into a follower? Let's look at the second fundamental to learn more.

Fundamental Two: Focus on Customers First by Creating Value

When an individual is browsing through social media, they are searching for things that provide them some sort of benefit. We would refer to this benefit simply as value. They are searching for valuable things to them. Different customers find different ideas valuable. For example, a serious businessman would find a blog article about improving office workflow to be of great value. A teenager would find a funny meme to be just as valuable to himself.

Value is what drives engagement. Followers do not engage with content that doesn't provide value to their lives. In other words, unless they are getting something out of the exchange, they won't care. There are a million other things on the internet that they could be looking at, so if it doesn't appeal to them in some way, they will ignore it.

Effective social media marketing requires that we develop a keen understanding of how to create and provide value to our followers. The reason for this is twofold:

1. If a customer finds your content to be valuable, they will follow you.
2. By providing them with something they need, you are signaling that you care about them.

Ineffective social media marketing tends to be highly self-focused. The assumption is that all one needs to do is post a few dozen times a week, all talking about your product or business and the job is done. However, this type of posting strategy doesn't work nearly as well as one would hope. Mainly because people are not interested in what you have to say about yourself, at least until they are interested in you. And the only way to get them interested in you is to provide them with some kind of incentive to pay attention.

Conversational narcissism must be avoided when it comes to social media marketing. It's all well and fine to make a post here and there about your company or products, but if those are the only types of content that you release, people will not take you too seriously.

Instead, you should work to identify what your consumer base values are. After that, you should work to aggregate and create content that reflect these values. Blog posts, articles, pictures and infographics are all excellent types of content that draw the viewer in and gets them to engage with you.

The more that you focus on your customers' needs and wants, the better chances you have of capturing their attention. And once you have their attention, you will be able to then show them your own products or services. In other words, to get what you want, you have to give them what they want. This is the give and take nature of social media. Everyone on Facebook or Instagram is looking for content that provides value to their lives.

Fundamental Three: Organic Marketing Has a Limit

Organic marketing is the process of marketing through the natural methods of using a social media platform. Making a post that is shown to 300 followers is organic marketing. It happens naturally and costs you nothing. When first getting started, organic marketing has quite the allure to it. The ability to gain customers without paying a dime sounds too good to be true. And in some ways, it is possible for you to generate customers and sales through organic marketing. The simple act of having a Facebook or Instagram page can bring in potential sales, especially if people are sharing your posts with their friends.

However, there are limits to your ability to market organically. The biggest limit is that all social media companies themselves, Facebook, Twitter, Instagram, are all interested in selling advertising space to companies. That is how these companies make money, they generate large user bases and then sell advertisers ad space to reach that user base.

This means that social media platforms have strong incentive to push business accounts towards paying for advertisements. They incentivize this behavior by limiting the amount that an organic, unpaid post can reach. For example, Facebook will limit your ability to reach followers when you post. You may have 1,000 followers, but your post will only show up in about 200 feeds. This is because Facebook doesn't want you using their services for free. They would rather that you pay a fee and promote your post instead, reaching all of your followers.

Ultimately, organic marketing has limitations. You can work for a while, growing your brand, increasing your following and generating sales through unpaid, organic marketing, but it won't nearly be as efficient as paid marketing. On top of that, organic marketing is slower and doesn't yield the same level of results that a highly targeted ad campaign would be. This isn't to say that there is no place for organic marketing, just that you shouldn't expect to be able to seriously market on social media without investing money in ads.

Fundamental Four: Social Media is a Means to an End, Not the End Itself

It can be easy to get caught up in focusing entirely on social media, especially since your task is to market through it. It's easy to get sucked into the idea of wanting to grow your social media pages as much as possible. Getting a lot of likes and page follows can be addicting, and if you're not careful, you could potentially lose sight of the purpose of social media marketing. Social media marketing isn't about increasing your popularity or growing your page, rather it is about helping customers move through a sales funnel, to the end step of making a conversion.

This means your main focus shouldn't be on simply increasing your popularity on any given platform, rather you should be focusing on developing a system of moving people through each step of the funnel. Social media platforms are incredible tools for creating awareness, excitement and desire for a product, but the goal is to eventually move your follower off of social media and onto a platform where you have full control.

Social media is inherently competitive when it comes to attention. A follower may be looking at your post one minute, but the next they may get a message or see another post and become distracted. You only have half of the customer's attention for as long as they are on the social media platform. On top of that, you also have to work with the confines and limitations that these platforms have. You don't have full control, which limits your ability to properly market your products and services.

Instead of looking at social media as the end goal, you should look at it as a means of capturing interest and generating awareness. Then, once that awareness and interest has been captured, social media can move these potential customers to your domain, where you will better be able to advertise to them.

To summarize, the fundamentals of social media marketing is creating relationships, providing followers with valuable content, realizing organic marketing has inherent limitations and that the ultimate end goal is to move customers to your own domains. These are the four basic building blocks to any successful social media marketing campaign. Whether you're using Facebook, Instagram or any other social media platform, these principles apply.

Create Valuable Content

Social media is powered by sharing content. They are looking for some kind of content that adds something to their lives. One of your primary jobs as a social media marketer is to create or aggregate valuable content, so that they can be shared through your chosen social media outlets.

This isn't a simple or easy task, but it is necessary. Content is king, as the old adage goes. As long as you are able to generate unique and valuable content for users, you will be able to capture interest, create leads and gain a following. Ultimately, you will be able to convert those followers into tribe members, especially if your content is good enough to keep them coming back for more and more.

Understanding Content Types:

At the core, content is meant to provide a solution to a customer's problem. In basic terms, the problem is that the customer needs something and the solution is the content you are providing. For example, a common problem is that a customer is bored. You solve that problem by providing content that entertains them. This is the primary way that you will foster connection with customers. Provide good content, gain a follower.

There are several different types of content, geared towards solving different problems. We can break them down into three basic categories: Entertainment, Information and Assistance.

Entertainment:

Entertainment is one of the most universal types of content that exists online. People are always looking for some kind of distraction from their problems and the real world. Entertainment often solves this problem by providing interesting and enjoyable experiences that make them smile, make them think or make them laugh. Entertainment content can be as simple as a picture of a cat with captions, or as complex as a long YouTube video.

Information:

Education is another extremely popular form of content. The internet has enabled people to learn just about anything out there and millions of people each day are scouring the internet, looking for information about their particular interests or niches. Providing high quality education and information content is a surefire way of developing a steady following.

Assistance:

Assistance is a type of content that is an offshoot of information. Rather than simply just providing information or education, assistance is where you generate content that actively works to solve their problem. This could be a how-to video, a step by step instructional blog post or a visual guide. Assistance content is extremely valuable because it shows that you care enough about your customers to provide them with free ways of solving their own problems.

Collecting Content:

There are two different ways that you can acquire content to be shared through social media. The first is to aggregate content, which means that you go online, find a bunch of pre-existing content that does not belong to you and then share it on your page.

Content aggregation is a perfectly fine strategy, provided that you give proper credit to the individuals who actually created the content. You can scour the internet, collect great content and share it with others, all without having to go through the process of creating the content yourself. This is a great way to fill the bulk of your posts with good, relevant content.

There are some downsides to content aggregation. The biggest is that this content won't play into your brand or direct people toward your websites. Rather, these pieces of content will exist simply as a means of generating interest in your profile. You may gain followers out of the deal, but you won't have the opportunity to direct them to your website.

The second type of content is original content, created and produced by you. Original content is extremely valuable, especially in social media platforms, where people often come across the same, unoriginal content over and over again.

Original content allows for you to present your company brand and direct people to your website through the inclusion of watermarks or even direct links to your domains. If people like your content and begin to share it, there is a chance that your content could bring in a wider array of viewers. This could potentially translate to an increased following or even conversions!

The downside to original content creation is that you have to spend time, effort and in some cases, money to be able to create that content. Content comes in all different shapes and sizes, but at the end of the day, it has to be created by hand. Let's take a look at the most popular types of content that can be created.

Blog Posts:

Long form written content remains to be one of the most popular types of content out there. People love to read articles. By utilizing a blog, you can generate blog posts that can then be dispersed through social media. This will achieve two major goals: creating awareness of your business and directing them to your website. Of course, they won't be visiting your website for any other reason than to see your blog, but you have a chance of converting them to at least following your blog for updates periodically. And once they have finished reading the post that interested them, they might poke around some more on your site, which could increase your chances of an organic sale.

Infographics:

Infographics are exceptionally popular because they combine strong visuals with information. People often enjoy reading infographics and are quick to share them, especially if they find them to be well made. Creating infographics does require both visual design skill as well as properly documented sources, which requires research time.

Pictures:

Memes, drawings, illustrations or simple photographs tend to be shared the most due to their simplicity. People can quickly glance at the content, get an understanding of it and then experience wonder, humor or excitement. While pictures most likely won't direct them to your website directly, they are still great ways to entertain your followers and provide them with the content that they care about.

Video:

Videos are another type of popular content that people like to engage with and share. We'll be covering this subject more in depth in the YouTube section, which is the primary outlet for not only creating videos, but also for sharing them through multiple social media platforms.

These four types of content make up what most social media users enjoy interacting with on a daily basis. As a social media marketer, you're going to want to have an established schedule of creating, collecting and releasing these types of content on your chosen platforms. The more content that you are able to release, the more your followers will engage.

It's important to remember that the content you're distributing isn't meant to promote or actively sell your products. Those types of posts aren't considered to be content, rather they are considered to be advertisements. While it's perfectly fine to sprinkle in an ad here or there in your posting schedule, you're going to want to focus primarily on releasing content that is for the benefit of your followers. This will help generate goodwill, increase their interest in your profile page and gain you followers.

Over time, the more people who engage with your content will become more receptive to the ads that you do end up posting. After all, you have proven to them that you genuinely do care about them by giving them the things that they want. This back and forth, give and take relationship are the backbone of a successful social media marketing strategy.

Chapter 2 Why my business needs social media?

At this point, not being present on social media is like flipping through a telephone book to find the number of your hairdresser. Or still owning a Nokia 3310. And while there is nothing wrong with using a two-decade-old cell phone model or keeping it old-school with hand-written telephone books, one thing is certain – those people miss out on the perks of today's technology. And that's perfectly fine. If you are just a guy who has a no-modern-technology principle, that is. But if you are a business that is looking for a way to increase the conversion and reap as many benefits as possible, then being present online is a must.

For many people social media is the internet, so they spend their hours scrolling down their social media platforms. Why? Because there is no reason to leave, actually. From chatting with people, to being up-to-date with news and finding and buying products and services, the social networks literally have it all. If you want your business to be successful, then having a strong social media presence is of great essence.

If your business is still not active on social media, then that is definitely the missing link that can strengthen the connection between your product/service and your customers. Still not sure whether it is worth the time and effort? Here are the benefits of being present on the social networks:

Web Traffic

Marketing your business on social media is a crucial part for your web traffic:

Posting on Social Media Drives Your Targeted Audience

Of course you want your business to be the first thing people will see when surfing the internet for similar products/services. But is that really possible if you are not active online? Posting regularly on social media will help you take domination over the first search page which will, in turn, increase your profits.

These social media posts are extremely valuable for increasing web traffic. For instance, think about what happens when you update your website. It surely takes a while for it to get traction with the search engines, right? That means that the number of customers that will be aware of your new content will be limited. Posting on social media will help your potential customers find your new content easily and then be re-directed to your website. This means that you don't have to wait for a customer to click on your website to find out your updates. Social media allows you to reach potential customers even if they are not looking to buy at that exact moment,

Social Media Posts Boosts the SEO

Search engine optimization is of great importance for your online presence and overall business. Don't be fooled that this is not that important. SEO experts know which sites have constant traffic and which sits lonely and forgotten. A great content strategy can obviously skyrocket your search rankings, however, social media posts also have the power to drive more traffic to your site. By re-sharing popular content you can easily optimize your page and lure existing and potential customers to take a peek. The boosted traffic will then lead to inbound clicks and will have a significant impact on your prominence in Google rankings.

Quoting Can Make You More Reachable

Sometimes, a simple quote can throw more traffic your way. Whether you have used a PR tool such as HARO to find experts for your site or you simply want to quote an expert with a strong influence on social media, this can surely help your business. Chances are, by quoting (and tagging!) an expert in your tweet or Facebook post, that person will most likely share or retweet your post which will help you reach potential customers from their list of followers and increase your site's traffic.

Connecting with Customers

Being the bridge that can connect the gap between you and your customers, social media is definitely the shortcut you need to take in order to reach your audience the fastest way possible.

Reaching Customers

Social media is perhaps the only tool that can help you reach customers from all age groups at once. These networks are not just for teenagers searching for entertainment. The social media platforms are actively used by more than 2.7 billion people, so it is safe to say that whatever your target audience is, your potential customers are spending some efficient time on social media already. In fact, a study has actually found that 37% of all the Americans over 65 years of age are social media users.

Whether you want to reach young adults, housewives, or retirees, social media is the best place to introduce your product/service to them.

Besides, advertising on social media allows targeting and retargeting your audience which can play a crucial role in your marketing strategy. For instance, the ads on Facebook can be filtered around the needs of your customers and target only the age, location, industry, etc. of the audience that you are trying to reach.

Learning about Your Target Audience

Perhaps the biggest reason why social media marketing is so game-changing for businesses is the fact that these networks actually allow you to have a real interaction with your existing and potential customers. This creates an incredible opportunity to peek inside your audience's lives and learn about the customer behaviors first-hand. By reading posts and tweets, you can easily find the answers to the questions that every business is mostly concerned with:

- What product/services do people want to buy and why?
- What kind of websites do people mostly visit?
- What are the biggest hobbies nowadays and how can my product/service help?
- What types of posts do people share the most?

Finding the answers to these questions will help you understand your customers and allow you to write compelling posts and tweets that people will find appealing. By retweeting and sharing, you will not only increase the traffic and eventually profits, but also pinpoint what are the disappointments of the customers and how to refine your product/service in order to increase conversion.

Getting Noticed Easily

Imagine that you are hosting an event. A decent promotion is kind of required, right? What best way to do it than to have an active social media presence? Social media platforms will help you spread the word which will not only bring more guests, but can also throw a few big perks your way such as finding donors that are eager to participate.

Improving Your Brand's Image

Marketing your product/service on social media can help you thrive as a company, increase the exposure of your brand, and make its image recognizable and trustworthy.

The Best Customer Service Tool

Building a great image for your brand starts with keeping your customers happy and content. Many studies have shown that customers mostly reward those companies that take the time to quickly respond to their inquiries. But quickly responding to complaints isn't what it used to be. If there is a customer request pending, they are expecting for the issue to be solved right away.

Social media helps you offer customer service that is quick, helpful, and proactive, and gives you the opportunity to reach and help your customers before they get the chance to call your call center. This little trick just saved British Telecom over 2 million pounds in customer service costs, so just let that sink in for a second.

Building Up the Loyalty of Your Brand

This is actually pretty self-explanatory, but it would be remiss not to mention it. By taking the time to engage with your customers actively and provide them with beneficial info, help with inquiries, and keep them entertained without asking a thing in return, your brand's loyalty is actually enhanced.

The right social media presence can bring value to the customers and show them that you are not looking to empty their pockets, but that you actually care whether they are satisfied with your product/service or not.

Chapter 3 Defining your audience

As we discussed earlier, defining your audience is essential to creating your own personal brand. It is the process of examining your body of work and what you have to offer, followed by an intense dive into market research and what it tells you about how well or poorly you and your content will sell among different demographics. Defining your audience also entails conducting your own personal research as well as introducing common sense into the equation. You do not have to pay a market research analyst money to figure out that your fashion blog geared towards LGBTQIA youth is not going to circulate well in the over 65 communities of Boca Raton, Florida. While every person is an individual and it can seem cold or even heartless and sociopathic to boil people down to demographics and age ranges and taste, but at the end of the day it is not going to be worth your limited time and resources to market to an entire community for the sake of reaching your snowflake consumer.

Defining your audience is also essential because as you may already know, once you have a defined your group of interest and best possible marketing opportunities, you can now begin to target that audience with your branding. This can mean running ads in media that you know members of your key demographic are likely to tune in to, as well as deciding to research the ways in which you can better serve the people who will hopefully become your financial supporters. Let us say, for example, that you are targeting men and women in their 30's and 40's who are interested in cooking. You create a cooking channel on YouTube and write a weekly blog about all things happening in the kitchen. Since you know who will be most likely to tune into your channel, read your blogs, and follow you on social media, you should consider what kinds of things people in this age range and demographic enjoy most. Your recipes are made from simple ingredients and sometimes premade things, so you know that your target audience is most likely people who work and do not have a great deal of time or money to spend on every meal, but still want to make them taste good and be nutritious. You could write several posts periodically about the importance of balancing time with quality preparation in the kitchen. You could make sure to use less professional techniques and make your videos easy to follow and recreate at home. You could partner with brands that are available in the lesser-expensive grocery stores when sponsoring products or having videos paid for.

Ultimately, defining your audience will help you to conduct a better, more targeted effort in your personal brand, and it simply involves identifying your audience, then getting to know them and the things that they value, then implementing that into your branding technique. You can even cater to your audience without compromising yourself in professional branding. Yes, it is somewhat more difficult to know what a potential employer wants as they do not publish market research reports on such things, but you can deduce what type of things they are looking for simply by getting to know more about the company. Read their website and memorize their company values. If you have the time, prior to an interview or submitting a resume, include some of those keywords into your social media posts. See what kinds of coworkers they have hired. Are there any common traits you see? Get to know what your potential employer wants to see and hear from an ideal candidate, and do your best to implement that into your own brand and delivery. Defining your audience is simply identifying who is most likely to buy what you are branding, and then giving them what they would like most. Learn to empathize with your audience and make them feel comfortable when taking in everything you have to offer.

Chapter 4 Using social media platforms for marketing

Dominating social media in actuality is going to require you to focus your social media platform with a clear approach, defined goals, and a strategy that will help you reach those goals. Creating a multi-platform approach requires you to know how to leverage each platform, how you can build a massive following on each platform, and then how to turn that platform into a working social media sales funnel. Before you can start creating your strategy and determining how to grow on each platform, you need to decide what your goals are and how you can best reach those goals using social media. Each platform is going to provide you with slightly different benefits. So, by identifying your goals first, you can ensure that you are going to be using the right platforms and enforcing the right strategies to maximize your time investment on social media.

Creating Your Business Goals
The first thing you want to do is create your business goals for these year. Typically, all of your other strategic goals should directly reflect your overall business goals. By knowing exactly what it is that you are trying to accomplish in your business in the immediate future, you can start creating goals for your social media platforms as well. You can set one or more goals for your business in the near future, though you should be intentional about setting only one or two goals as your primary focus for the year. This way, you are clear on exactly what it is that you are working toward and you can design every secondary goal and strategy around that primary goal in your business.

The best way to create your business goal is to look at what means the most to you and your business for the coming year and create your goals around that concept. If you are brand new in business, you might set the goal to make your first year profitable in business. Identify what exact number that would be for you. Or, you might set the goal to increase your brand awareness and start connecting with a broader audience so that you have a system of trusted people to invest in your business as you continue to grow your brand name and popularity over the years to come. If you have been in business longer, your goal may be to refocus your brand on something slightly different and bring your audience along on that adjustment with you. You might try to increase your profits this year so that you can hire more employees or offer more to your audience.

Whatever your goals may be, make sure that you use the S.M.A.R.T planning goal style to ensure that you are setting goals that you can actually achieve this same year. So, your goals need to be specific, measurable, attainable, realistic, and timely. For example, rather than saying "I want to earn a six-figure year in these year " you could say "I want to earn $125,000 in revenue by December 31, of these year through my business." When you set specific goals, it becomes easier for you to know whether or not you are effectively moving toward your goals. This way you can determine if your strategies are working or if they need to be adjusted to help you advance more effectively.

Creating Your Social Media Goals
Once you have your general business goals created, you can start determining what your social media goals are going to be. It is important to realize that social media works differently for different business models. Approaching your social media goals requires you to consider what exactly

social media can do for you and how you can maintain your image while incorporating social media into your strategy. For example, if you are a lawyer, you may not want to use social media as openly as another business because you cannot freely share certain information. In certain industries, you will need to be more conservative in your approach, which means that your goals should reflect these conservative social media values. So, if you were a lawyer on Instagram, rather than being open and sharing snippets of your life online, you would likely refrain from using stories or IGTV altogether and instead simply create posts on your feed. These posts should be targeted specifically toward your desired audience by providing them with the information that they need to know, then direct them to your website or your phone number so that you can talk privately with them. In this scenario, your social media goals would be to entirely get people to contact you, rather than to build a massive following and become a well-liked influencer in your industry.

You can determine which style of social media goals you need quite simply. If you run a more professional business where you need to keep a large portion of information private, then you need to use social media to drive people to contact you. If you run a brick and mortar store, then you need to use social media to drive people into your store so that they can shop with you. If you run an online business, then you need to build your following so that you can market to a larger audience.

That being said, you still need to be more specific when you are setting social media goals. What *exactly* are you trying to achieve through social media? For example, if you are the owner of a coffee shop, do you want to drive more tourists to your coffee shop so that they can take pictures with your photo ops and increase the popularity of your shop? Or, do you want to increase the amount of local individuals who are coming through your doors to purchase coffee and become loyal visitors? If you are an influencer, maybe you want to increase your following so that you can generate pitches for popular brands and start earning more income through your platform.

Whatever it is that you desire to do, make sure that you are utilizing social media as a tool in your overall goals and not relying on it as the exclusive strategy itself. Even if social media is your primary method for reaching out to your audience, you should recognize that your business itself is not exclusive to social media. You will still have plenty of other things that need to happen in order for you to achieve your goals. When you see social media as a tool and organize it into your overall strategy as a tool, you put yourself in the position where you can start using social media as one of your most powerful forces online.

Determining What Platforms Will Work Best for You
After determining what your goals are for social media, you have one last thing that you need to consider before beginning the process of designing your social media strategy. You need to determine what platforms are going to be the most effective for you when it comes to achieving the goals that you have set out to achieve. In each of the following sections, you are going to learn about the six biggest social media platforms that presently exist, how they can be used, and who will most benefit from them. Make sure that you read through this information and choose platforms that are actually going to support you in achieving your goals so that you are focusing your efforts in areas that make sense to your overall goals and business.

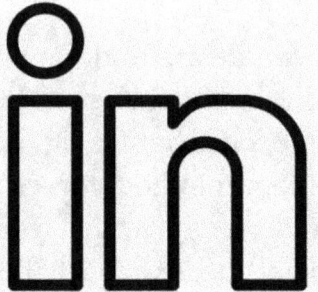

Chapter 5 Social media strategy

Creating Your Goals

Dominating social media in 2019 is going to require you to focus your social media platform with a clear approach, defined goals, and a strategy that will help you reach those goals. Creating a multi-platform approach requires you to know how to leverage each platform, how you can build a massive following on each platform, and then how to turn that platform into a working social media sales funnel. Before you can start creating your strategy and determining how to grow on each platform, you need to decide what your goals are and how you can best reach those goals using social media. Each platform is going to provide you with slightly different benefits. So, by identifying your goals first, you can ensure that you are going to be using the right platforms and enforcing the right strategies to maximize your time investment on social media.

Creating Your Business Goals

The first thing you want to do is create your business goals for 2019. Typically, all of your other strategic goals should directly reflect your overall business goals. By knowing exactly what it is that you are trying to accomplish in your business in 2019, you can start creating goals for your social media platforms as well. You can set one or more goals for your business in 2019, though you should be intentional about setting only one or two goals as your primary focus for the year. This way, you are clear on exactly what it is that you are working toward and you can design every secondary goal and strategy around that primary goal in your business.

The best way to create your business goal is to look at what means the most to you and your business for the coming year and create your goals around that concept. If you are brand new in business, you might set the goal to make your first year profitable in business. Identify what exact number that would be for you. Or, you might set the goal to increase your brand awareness and start connecting with a broader audience so that you have a system of trusted people to invest in your business as you continue to grow your brand name and popularity over the years to come. If you have been in business longer, your goal may be to refocus your brand on something slightly different and bring your audience along on that adjustment with you. You might try to increase your profits this year so that you can hire more employees or offer more to your audience.

Whatever your goals may be, make sure that you use the S.M.A.R.T planning goal style to ensure that you are setting goals that you can actually achieve in 2019. So, your goals need to be specific, measurable, attainable, realistic, and timely. For example, rather than saying "I want to earn a six-figure year in 2019" you could say "I want to earn $125,000 in revenue by December 31, 2019 through my business." When you set specific goals, it becomes easier for you to know whether or not you are effectively moving toward your goals. This way you can determine if your strategies are working or if they need to be adjusted to help you advance more effectively.

Creating Your Social Media Goals
Once you have your general business goals created, you can start determining what your social media goals are going to be. It is important to realize that social media works differently for different business models. Approaching your

social media goals requires you to consider what exactly social media can do for you and how you can maintain your image while incorporating social media into your strategy. For example, if you are a lawyer, you may not want to use social media as openly as another business because you cannot freely share certain information. In certain industries, you will need to be more conservative in your approach, which means that your goals should reflect these conservative social media values. So, if you were a lawyer on Instagram, rather than being open and sharing snippets of your life online, you would likely refrain from using stories or IGTV altogether and instead simply create posts on your feed. These posts should be targeted specifically toward your desired audience by providing them with the information that they need to know, then direct them to your website or your phone number so that you can talk privately with them. In this scenario, your social media goals would be to entirely get people to contact you, rather than to build a massive following and become a well-liked influencer in your industry.

You can determine which style of social media goals you need quite simply. If you run a more professional business where you need to keep a large portion of information private, then you need to use social media to drive people to contact you. If you run a brick and mortar store, then you need to use social media to drive people into your store so that they can shop with you. If you run an online business, then you need to build your following so that you can market to a larger audience.

That being said, you still need to be more specific when you are setting social media goals. What *exactly* are you trying to achieve through social media? For example, if you are the owner of a coffee shop, do you want to drive more tourists to your coffee shop so that they can take pictures with your photo ops and increase the popularity of your shop? Or, do you want to increase the amount of local individuals who are coming through your doors to purchase coffee and become loyal visitors? If you are an influencer, maybe you want to increase your following so that you can generate pitches for popular brands and start earning more income through your platform.

Whatever it is that you desire to do, make sure that you are utilizing social media as a tool in your overall goals and not relying on it as the exclusive strategy itself. Even if social media is your primary method for reaching out to your audience, you should recognize that your business itself is not exclusive to social media. You will still have plenty of other things that need to happen in order for you to achieve your goals. When you see social media as a tool and organize it into your overall strategy as a tool, you put yourself in the position where you can start using social media as one of your most powerful forces online.

Determining What Platforms Will Work Best for You

After determining what your goals are for social media, you have one last thing that you need to consider before beginning the process of designing your social media strategy. You need to determine what platforms are going to be the most effective for you when it comes to achieving the goals that you have set out to achieve. In each of the following sections, you are going to learn about the six biggest social media platforms that presently exist, how they can be used, and who will most benefit from them. Make sure that you read through this information and choose platforms that are actually going to support you in achieving your goals so that you are focusing your efforts in areas that make sense to your overall goals and business.

Harmful Risks "Experts" Tell You

With the rise of the social media empire, unfortunately, there are many "experts" out there who are sharing harmful myths about social media marketing and how people can utilize social media platforms to build a strong presence for their brand. These "experts" tend to be quite persuasive, which can lead to many individuals following them only to find themselves being fed bad information that stops them from being able to grow the online presence that they desire.

Before you get started creating your official strategies and getting your brand online, it is important that you understand what these myths are and how they can negatively impact your business if you are not careful. Chances are, you have already heard at least one of these myths which is why it is important that you learn the truth first, to avoid having you go into the process of building your online brand while believing this information to be true.

Myth #1: Social Media Analytics Are Not Important
The first big myth that many self-proclaimed experts will tell you is that your analytics are not important. This myth comes through in two ways. One states that as long as you are getting "some" engagement on each post, you are doing well, the other states that even if you are getting no engagement, people are still seeing your posts. These myths obviously come from people who do not understand social media marketing or the purpose of social media marketing.

Analytics on social media tell you exactly what people like, what they want more of, and how you can share with them in a way that actually creates traction and success in your brand. When you look at your analytics, you can see exactly what posts people are enjoying the most, and you can emulate these posts to begin making even more success in your online platform. You *want* to be doing this because, in doing so, you can ensure that you are actually being seen by the right people. If your posts are not getting enough traction or if your engagement is not regularly growing, it is because you are missing a step or doing something wrong. As long as you are listening to what your audience likes by paying attention to the analytics, there is no reason why your online platform should not be growing on a consistent basis.

In regard to whether or not "no engagement" means that your posts are still being "seen," this is simply not how social media works. Posts that are not engaged with are hidden from timelines as social media platforms will assume that these posts are irrelevant and that they are simply cluttering up individuals' newsfeeds. People like to see posts that are relevant or interesting and since social media caters to its users, it will favor showing these posts over any other posts. That means, if you have posts that are regularly being ignored, it is likely because no one is seeing them; not because they "are seeing them but are afraid to engage for fear of being sold to" as many perceived experts will attempt to tell you.

Myth #2: Social Media Is Only for Creating New Customers

If you have ever heard that social media is specifically meant for gaining new customers, then you have heard another common myth in the social media marketing world. The truth is, social media is not exclusively for creating new customers, it is also for retaining customers. In fact, a recent study showed that 84% of most brands on Facebook are being followed by people who were customers *first* and who went on to find them on social media, not by new customers who have never shopped with the brand at all.

This statistic likely varies across all of the different platforms, but the fact remains that social media is a powerful tool for staying in touch with your existing audience and maintaining their loyalty. When you encourage your existing customers to follow you, you create the opportunity to maintain and grow your relationship with them, which supports you in bringing existing customers back and turning them into loyal fans of your brand.

In fact, when you are on social media, you should be targeting your existing audience as much as you target your new audience, since your existing audience will be the ones already prepared to share their experiences of their company with others. If you cater to them and connect with them online, this makes it easier for them to share their reviews of your brand with their friends and family, and hopefully, drive more attention to your brand and traffic to your business. For that reason, you should be targeting your existing audience often and create a platform that is just as enjoyable for them to follow as it is for new followers to find you.

Myth #3: Ignore Negative Feedback or Commentary

Receiving negative feedback or comments on your brand can be hurtful, especially if you are closely connected with your company or if you are your own brand. Hearing what other people are saying, especially when what they are saying is not nice, can feel like a deep and painful insult and it can make running your own business challenging.

Initially, you may even feel like leaving the social media world to avoid having a platform for negative feedback like this to come in, though that would not be effective in helping you reach the people you desired. If you look around on the net, a common statement made by self-proclaimed social media experts is that you should simply ignore negative commentary and feedback because engaging with "trolls" is not helpful to your business.

However, this is actually an extremely negative way to handle negative commentary and it can lead to your business and brand being viewed as ignorant or even suspicious. As well, when you ignore the negative commentary, you assume that everyone who has something bad to say is a "troll" or someone who is trying to bash your company when, in reality, it may just be someone who previously liked your company but encountered a bad experience. In other words, you could use this as an opportunity to change someone's mind about your brand and build a loyal follower if you play your cards right. Even if you can't, and the person truly is just someone who has nothing nice to say, not handling the situation effectively can make other potentially interested customers less interested in your brand.

The best way to handle negative commentary is to kindly respond back thanking the individual for leaving feedback, apologizing for their negative experience, and offering a solution to rectify it. Or, if the comment was left by someone who is not your client, you might consider responding kindly to let them know that you see and hear them, that you appreciate their concerns, and that you will rectify the situation as appropriate.

Here are three examples of different types of comments that you might experience online and ways that you can kindly and appropriately handle them. Notice that each strategy puts you on the record as being a company that listens, cares, and serves rather than one that simply ignores people and their problems.

Comment #1:
Follower: "In the past I used (company) products until, I purchased one of their new [products] and the quality was really bad! It broke within the first week. The quality of this [company] has really gone downhill since the beginning. Shame, too. They used to be so good!"

You: "Hi [follower]! We are so sorry to hear about your negative experience, that is definitely not what we want! I can assure you that quality is still a priority when it comes to the products we create. Can you please contact us at [customer care info] so we can rectify your experience?"

Comment #2:
Follower: "I heard this company is horrible, my friend tried their products and felt ripped off. I will never waste my money here!"

You: "Hi [follower]! We are so sorry to hear that your friend had a negative experience. We pride ourselves in offering high quality products to our clients. Do you know if your friend contacted our customer care team to receive support in rectifying the situation? We would love to pass this along to our quality control department to ensure that this does not happen again."

Comment #3:
Follower: "Nice try! I've seen products like this before, they're a complete waste. Don't spend your money on something like this!"

You: "Hi [follower]! We're sorry to hear that you will not be giving our products a try because you think these products are a waste. Not all companies create [this product] equally, so you might be surprised to learn that ours stands out due to its [highlight points.] We hope you'll give it a try!"

When you handle comments properly, you show existing customers that you care and that you want them to have a positive experience, and you show new customers that you are not simply trying to make money through unethical or illegitimate sales strategies. Since there are so many companies on the internet, setting yourself apart from others is imperative to let your audience know that you are a genuine company that stands in alignment with integrity and high-quality products. This way, people will be more likely to shop with you because they trust that if they have a negative experience for any reason that you will support them in rectifying that experience.

Myth #4: "Blank" Is Dead
Every single year, blog posts and other articles report that a certain platform is "dead" or is falling off the face of the map. This marketing strategy has been used for years to try and capture attention, drive people away from certain platforms, and gain followers on others. The truth is, no online platform has truly died unless no one is using it anymore.

Instead, these reports are often being shared by people who are using the wrong platforms, and therefore, are unable to connect with their desired audience. As a result, they believe said platform is dead when in reality, they are simply not utilizing the right platforms in the right ways to gain access to their audience.

If you read posts like this, take a moment to read through the active statistics of the platform that is claimed to have "died" because in most cases, these statistics will prove that the platform is not going anywhere. These are just another example of false marketing experts attempting to create traction in their business by creating clickbait content that holds no value or fact. Avoid marketers or experts who use claims like these, as they will likely lead you astray from the truth. Also, they may not be able to give you the proper guidance that you need to generate success in the online space.

Myth #5: If It's Not Selling, It's Not Marketing
At one time, most individuals who were using social media were marketing by sharing advertisement-looking posts repeatedly with an attempt to share products and services with their audiences. Since social media was so young and new at the time, these strategies worked and many people made a lot of money using these strategies. However, this strategy no longer works. Ultimately, too many people started using it and most followers grew to feel like they were reading through magazines filled with advertisements rather than social media timelines that were intended to connect loved ones and friends over the internet.

These days, the best way to build your business online is to focus on the social aspect of social media first and then tie in your sales after. There is a rule that suggests that you share your marketing content using an 80/20 rule, where you share 80% personal content and 20% sales posts so that people can get to know you more often than they are being sold to by you. This strategy is known as "attraction marketing" and it happens to be one of the most powerful strategies in today's online marketplace.

The reason why this strategy works, especially if you are running an exclusively online business, is because you are putting your relationships with others above your sales numbers. When people see this, they start feeling connected to you and they personally care about you and the message that you are sharing with your audience. They feel a sense of trust and understanding which leads to them feeling passionate about what you do and who you are, which helps them become people who are openly willing and eager to purchase from you when you do market your products to your audience.

So, just because every single post does not end with a sales pitch does not mean that it is not marketing. It simply means that some of your posts are marketing your brand and building brand awareness, and others are actually asking for sales and inviting people to buy into your product or services. In this day and age, this strategy is far more effective and productive than any other strategy. So, do not believe anyone who tries to tell you that you must somehow twist every single post into a sales pitch. This is simply not true.

Chapter 6 The Personal Reality of Personal Branding

Before digging into the mechanisms of what it takes to develop a personal brand, first, it is a good idea to explore what a personal brand truly is so that you can decide whether or not you are ready to have one. Even if you already have a brand, if you are struggling to grow at the rate which you desire, reading this chapter will help you equip yourself with the right tools to approach your personal growth effectively. Personal branding is all the rage right now and, in one way or another, many people use it as a tool to develop their reputations and leverage their reputation to earn better opportunities in life. That being said, some people personally brand by leveraging their reputation to gain more in life, and people who brand as an intentional tool that helps them develop a profitable business. If you are reading this book, the chances are that you want to develop your very own profitable business by leveraging your brand, which is an incredible idea!

Before you get started, understanding what it takes out of you as a person to run your brand is important. Many people start their businesses with a lack of awareness regarding the development of their brand on a personal level. Of course, the way these particular brands develop is different from your average brand because they are based on you as a person, rather than a separate entity that you have developed for your brand itself. For that reason alone, there is plenty of personal work, commitment, and effort that goes into creating your brand. Ideally, you should be prepared to take on all of this personal work to allow yourself to grow into the fullest potential of your personal brand and truly make the most out of your efforts. In this chapter, you are going to explore what these things are, how they may impact you, and what you can do to ensure that you grow through them rather than find yourself feeling trapped or stuck under a difficult mountain of growth.

Keep Your Mind Open

When it comes to personal branding, you must keep an open mind if you are going to grow through all of the obstacles that you will face along the way. Personal branding may be straight forward on paper, but when it comes to applying what you have learned, you will need to discover how you can mentally stay on track to continue applying the steps day after day. For someone who has never been in branding before, it can take some time to "learn the ropes" and discover how you are going to get yourself out there and grow. For some people, developing a brand is largely about having freedom, which can lead to a lack of work ethic and an inability to stay committed, and for others, it is easy to stay focused and keep working away. If you find that you are someone who struggles to stay focused, you will need to keep your mind open to learn about new ways that you can continue applying yourself, even when it feels challenging to stay committed.

Another reason why you want to keep an open mind is that developing your brand can be challenging if you stay too attached to your original idea. You need to have a strong vision for what you want to create, while also remaining flexible in how it looks and the steps that you will take to get there. To put it simply, you do not know everything right now, and as you learn and develop your brand more, your vision will evolve over time. Keeping an open mind will allow you to continue developing your brand so that you can easily allow yourself to continue building without attempting to confine yourself to a dream that may no longer fit your needs or desires.

Always Focus on Your Personal Growth

When it comes to developing a personal brand, personal growth is important. People who follow you are going to be genuinely engaged in your personal growth journey, regardless of what industry you are in, because your growth will inspire their growth. The more you focus on your personal growth, the more you are going to show up for and serve your audience, which allows everyone to continue growing together. Do not be afraid to endure the growth that naturally arises on your path, as well as the growth that you feel called to explore along the way, as all forms of personal growth will only help you reinforce the power of your brand.

In addition to helping your audience relate with you and feel inspired, personal growth will also help you develop a stronger brand in general. When you continually work toward personal growth, your confidence and abilities increase as well, which makes it easier for you to continue showing up and serving your audience. Not only will your increased self-confidence support your brand, but it will also support your entire life in general as you can begin enjoying more of your life and more of yourself through your personal development.

Keep Your Goals Clear

When it comes to personal branding, it can be challenging to identify what parts of yourself should be associated with your visible brand and what parts should be kept to yourself. On the one hand, you want to stay authentic and share your true self with your audience, whereas on the other hand, you want to make sure that you are not confusing them by sharing too much or getting off-brand. The best way to make sure that you are always staying on-brand with your audience is to make sure that you are clear in the goals that you have with your personal brand. If you are interested in sharing your brand with your audience so that you can teach them about marketing, then make sure that all of the parts of your personal self that you share with them in one way or another pertains to marketing. If you are developing a health and wellness brand as a personal trainer, make sure that the visible elements of your brand all coincide with your health and wellness commitments. The clearer you are with your brand development, the easier it is going to be for you to know exactly what you should be sharing, and what you should not be sharing.

In addition to having goals for your brand, do not forget to have goals for yourself, too. When it comes to developing a personal brand, it can be easy to forget that you have other aspects of your life beyond the life that you are building around your brand in the online space. Having personal goals can keep you more active in your personal life so that you can continue developing as an individual alongside developing your brand, which will further improve your chances at success.

Give Yourself Permission to Evolve

When you develop a personal brand, it can be easy to grow attached to the image that you have developed for your brand and then struggle to allow yourself to evolve over time. Many people find themselves unwilling to evolve their brand because they fear that their audience will stop following them through the changes. The reality is actually quite different: virtually every personal brand evolves over time, and in most cases, all of their loyal followers will simply evolve with them and continue to support the brand through all of the different evolutions. Some of your audience may fall off along the way, but trust that as they fall off, even more aligned members from your audience will begin arriving for you to serve them.

It is important for your overall health that you allow evolution to be a necessary staple in your brand, as no one wants to remain the same forever. Attempting to remain the same forever will cause you to lose your authenticity, which will result in your brand falling apart and you losing interest in what it is that you are trying to develop. For some business owners, this can even become a point of significant mental stress as they no longer permit themselves to be who they are, but instead attempt to remain the same in order to serve their audience. Trust that your evolution is a valuable asset to your brand, and continue working toward your evolution consistently, while also allowing it to be an important part of the brand that you are developing. The more you work together with yourself and your audience through evolution, the more authentic your brand will stay along the way.

Be Willing to Learn New Things

A part of personal development and evolution is being willing to learn new things, and this is especially important when it comes to developing a brand. When you are developing a brand, make sure that you are open to learning all of the new elements that come with the process, such as the mindset and technical strategies that are required. Do not be afraid to put yourself out there and learn a new skill if it is going to help you develop your brand faster.

At first, much of what goes into developing a brand needs to be done by you—unless you plan on hiring people to support you with everything. Even still, you should be developing your brand for you, as developing it in any other way could result in your brand not coming across as authentic or interesting. If you want to increase your chances at being recognized by your target audience, learning how to develop your social media accounts, website, and message in general is vital. Not only is this going to help you develop your brand with your message, but it also empowers you to run your brand your way so that even if you cannot afford to hire anyone for help, you can still develop all of the working parts of your brand yourself. Do not be afraid to take courses, or read books like this one, on social media marketing and the like to support you in developing your brand in the online space.

Learn to Let Go

When it comes to developing your online brand, you also need to learn to let go. Letting go may be one of the most powerful tools that you learn when it comes to developing your personal brand, as it will allow you to keep your brand moving forward even in the face of adversity. Two of the most important times that you need to pay attention to letting go is when it comes to letting go of the things mean people say, and letting go of your need to be perfect. Criticism and perfectionism are two of the more challenging things to work through when it comes to developing your business, and learning to let go is a major key for allowing you to overcome both of these things.

Many people find that having criticism toward their brand is challenging because they feel like they are being attacked personally, which is rarely true. When it comes to criticism, you need to understand that in most cases, people are only criticizing your services, not you, and they are rarely criticizing you in a way that is intended to be harsh or mean.

Instead, they are simply trying to provide you with feedback, and they may not necessarily have the skills required to provide positive feedback.

When it comes to letting go of perfectionism, this strategy is a powerful way to help you get your content out there sooner, rather than later. One thing that many people do is hold themselves back because they want everything to look perfect, which is rarely important to anyone other than themselves. Attempting to hold yourself up to standards of perfectionism can lead to you being afraid to move forward with anything because you will always be looking for flaws in your work. While you want to be proud of what you do, aim to have high standards, not perfect standards. Attempting to do everything perfectly will only result in you feeling as though you are not good enough, which may lead to you feeling unworthy of running your business. Do not be afraid to let go of perfectionism so that you can develop your business to the best of your abilities, and trust that your skills will evolve and improve as you grow.

Chapter 7 Don't be too professional

Professionalism is important for making your channel look like a big deal and something worth viewing, but this shouldn't make you lose touch with reality. It is important to always stay grounded and relevant to your audience. While viewers appreciate well-produced, high quality videos, they also want the content to be relatable and fun. For instance, there are plenty of very professional business executives in the television business. These executives wear suits and look professional in every way, including their physical appearance. They also have years, sometimes decades, of experience creating well-produced and high-quality programming on television. However, most viewers today, and definitely the younger audience, will say that there is nothing that ruins a television show faster than network executives getting too involved in the production of the shows they love. To put it plainly, these executives are the perfect embodiment of professionalism but that professionalism doesn't help them relate to or understand an audience and what they want to see. It is important that no matter what level of production your channel is able to reach that you don't forget what really made you popular to begin with, and this is always going to be your content and likeability.

One of the most common criticisms of YouTube channels after they succeed is that they forget what made them popular to begin with and in a sense they sell out. While this isn't the biggest concern you need to have when your channel hasn't even become popular yet, it is important to remember when your channel does finally and hopefully takes off. Growing your channel is the first step, but you could just as easily lose all of that growth in a short amount of time if you don't remain grounded and relatable to your audience. This doesn't mean you should be unprofessional, but don't become one of the talking suits that so routinely interferes with and ruins good content in television and movies either.

Chapter 8 Facebook Marketing

The Facebook Platform

What Is Facebook?
Facebook is arguably the most famous social media platform of this age. It is basically a channel that a lot of people make use of when they want to share photos and videos. It is also a trusted way to connect with old friends.

Although the general belief is that Mark Zuckerberg created Facebook, he did not do it alone. He created the platform alongside some colleagues from Harvard, namely Andrew McCollum, Eduardo Saverin, Chris Hughes, and Dustin Moskovitz. After its creation, Facebook was launched in 2004.

Their initial plan was for it to help Harvard students communicate with each other. Sometime later, it became "a thing" in other nearby universities as well. Two years after the launch, lots of teenagers became owners of accounts on Facebook. Now, there are over a billion accounts on this website.

How Does Facebook Work?
Signing up on Facebook is very easy. You can do so from its homepage, for one. As soon as you provide answers to their personal questions and fill in your age, the next step is to find your friends among the Facebook users out there. There are various ways to go about this. You can either let the platform have access to your contact list or search for people you know by name.

Before doing the latter, though, it is essential to complete your profile. It will make it easy for your friends, family members, and acquaintances to recognize you and accept your friend request. You can post pictures, links, videos or anything you wish to share with everyone. It can be on your timeline or that of a friend. Anything you post will be visible on the news feed of your friends regardless of where you make the post.

What Is Facebook News Feed?

Facebook's News Feed comprises a collection of stories that gets updated regularly. It occupies your home page's center after logging in. Here, you will see photos, links, videos, status updates, likes, app activities, groups, and pages that your friends uploaded on the platform.

Facebook chooses the posts that appear on your feed. It is mainly dependent on your activities there, as well as the users that make up your friends list. Hence, there is a huge likelihood that you will come across stories about stuff that you have searched for in the past. They may be recommended by your friends and from the groups that you visit often. If something receives lots of likes and comments, it will appear at the top of the News Feed.

Although this feature follows a chronological order when showing posts, it does not mean that the most recent ones will be seen before the older posts. It is up to you to tweak the settings to get the type of content you want on your feed. You may rely on Facebook tutorials to achieve that as well.

Devices That Allow You to Access Facebook

Facebook is accessible on virtually every device that can connect to the internet. So, you can use tablets, smartphones, laptops, etc. The fact that Facebook can be accessed by any device that connects to the internet is truly amazing. However, even more amazing is the fact that

Facebook is free. To get the best out of Facebook, merely get the Facebook app.

What Facebook Features Are Available to Users?

Marketplace

Marketplace on Facebook is similar to eBay or Craigslist. It is a section that's set aside for the purchase and sale of a commodity by account holders aged 18 years old and above.

When looking to buy goods using the marketplace, you can either look for the exact item you need or browse randomly for commodities near you. Usually, every item for sale comes with a price tag. Nevertheless, you can decide to offer to pay for something at a lower price.

On the marketplace, you can get lots of stuff, including antique vehicles, new or used clothes, etc. You can send the payment through an electronic process that doesn't require users to exit the Facebook platform.

Groups

A Facebook group is no different from a virtual forum on other sites. People with the same interests can have discussions in one about the things that they have in common.

The idea is that anyone can create a group on Facebook. There are three types of groups on Facebook. These are the open, closed, and secret groups. Each group will be explained in another section.

Town Hall

With town hall, you can stay connected to officials of your local government. You not only have the freedom to get in touch with them but also decide to follow their Facebook page. Furthermore, you can go ahead to include a constitute badge. It makes it possible for your identification as a resident in a specific district.

Messenger

If you enjoy chatting, then Facebook has a feature called Messenger that can be used to chat up individuals and groups. You can also play games and make calls with it. To access Messenger on your computer, open your profile. On the home page, click on the messages tab on the top navigation panel. It will take you to a new page where you can start a new conversation or continue a conversation with your friends.

Pages

Facebook Pages gives you the opportunity to reach more people on the platform. Its function is similar to that of the regular profiles. If an individual or a firm has a page, they can share videos, photos, links, and updates on it. Their difference is that when you share anything on a Facebook page, it is only seen by your followers. Hence, public figures, celebrities, firms, and organizations usually take advantage of this feature.

There are no restrictions on the creation of pages on Facebook. If you need to promote anything, you can make one that's dedicated to it. In case you have started a band, for instance, or you are handling a business project, you might consider creating a Facebook page. Nevertheless, for firms and celebrities, the process is merely open to their representatives.

Live Audio

The live audio feature that Facebook offers is perfectly suitable for individuals who enjoy being on air but may not have a platform yet. Anyone who connects to live audio through the feed can give feedback and share it with their Facebook contacts.

Events

Are you planning to make or attend an event? Do you want to know if any of your friends will be at a concert? Do you wish to invite people as soon as possible? Well, you don't have any reason to worry since Facebook has a dedicated feature for that.

With the platform's event section, you can discover happenings that will take place close to your location. When events are created on the platform, there are options for people to indicate if they will be attending or not. It, therefore, makes it possible for the host to come up with an effective plan for their guests. Furthermore, you can find events created by people you know.

There is no limit when it comes to the kinds of occasions you can announce on Facebook. The organization is open to everyone who has an account in the channel. Also, as the creator of an event, it is up to you to determine who can and cannot see it.

Live Video

Facebook live video is pretty much the visual counterpart of the website's live audio function. With the former, you can choose to stream a video real-time. Your fans on the page can share a link to it as well even while you are still on. They can also react and comment on it as the video plays.

Thus, Facebook live video is an ideal setting for question-and-answer segments with your fans. You can also decide to ante up the streaming experience by adding stickers and even scribbling on your video.

Creating a Facebook Account

On Facebook, there are two types of accounts you can create: a personal profile or fan/business page. Below are some tips when creating such accounts.

Facebook Profile

Of the two types of Facebook accounts, the most common is the Facebook profile. It is ideal for individuals who use the platform for leisure purposes.

With a personal profile, you can post everything you want, e.g., details about your workplace or the institutions you have attended. You may also connect with people that you met a long time ago.

There is no difficulty in coming up with this account type. The registration is no different from the process that you have carried out on other platforms in the past. You merely have to provide the following information:

- First and last name
- Email and phone number
- Desired password
- Gender and date of birth

As soon as these data are correctly filled, you can click on the "Create an Account" button.

Personalizing Your Facebook Profile

If you are looking to personalize your profile on Facebook, there are procedures you can follow.

1. Select a profile picture that will represent who you are on Facebook. Adding one makes it easy for everyone to recognize you and contact you.

2. Go ahead and look for friends. You can search for friends on Facebook using their name, email ID or mobile number.

3. You can decide who can access your Facebook profile by making it private. When you have an account on the platform, after all, you are naturally putting Facebook in charge of your personal information. Hence, it is vital to set boundaries from the beginning by changing things up on Settings.

At this point, you can now interact with your acquaintances and friends. You can also receive notifications about events happening around you.

Facebook Page

Apart from having a personal account on Facebook, you can have a professional page that can also serve as your online store. There are two options available here.

Brand or Business

It is a method that ensures an increase in your business' online reach. It will help you get noticed by more potential customers.

Public Figure or Community

You can also open a Facebook community where you can make your interests known. It is an ideal way to get music, sports news, show updates, and other forms of content out in public.

To start, you need to open a personal Facebook account. The business page varies from the latter, however, because you have to be careful in selecting a suitable name so that your prospective clients can find you easily.

Once done, you have to select an excellent profile picture and cover photo. You may add details about your products as well if you intend to run a store online.

Mistakes on Facebook

Running a business page or group on Facebook means you will need to run some ads on the platform. If you fail to follow the guidelines on the platform, Facebook will not let you run any ad. Your ads may perform poorly if you don't set it up correctly.

Before running a Facebook ad campaign, it is crucial to know how to advertise on the platform. For instance, you should learn about policies that may affect the approval of your advertisements, as well as mistakes that you might make due to your inexperience. It will also be helpful to read about other successful advertisers on the platform to know how they function.

Numerous opportunities for business growth appear when you open a Facebook account. Establish your authority and enhance your organic reach with this free platform.

Strategies for Your Posts

Facebook is fundamentally based on posts and their ability to go 'viral' – which means that your content has to be so encapsulating that it draws people in. Here are some strategies for viral Facebook posts:

Use Emotions

Facebook is not really about selling products – it's about actually connecting with people. You can't connect with people unless you are selling emotions. It doesn't really matter what your product is — on Facebook, if you want people to care about your page and your brand, you have to connect with them emotionally.

The only way you can connect with people is by associating the utility of your product with things that make people relate to it. So, if you're trying to sell, say clothes, you can't just show people what you offer and hope that they wear it. If you instead put up a story of how your clothes are made and showcase the people who work endlessly to ensure that the clothes you make are perfect, you're far more likely to gain public attention.

Don't Overdo It

Of course, trying to connect with your potential audience is important, but make sure that you're not trying too hard. If you latch on to every new trend and joke around too much, it's eventually going to saturate your audience. Also, many brands think they can connect to the younger generation by using their slang and style, but try not to partake in silly things like this. It's only going to make your posts seem fake, and as though you're trying to be relatable just for the sake of it.

It's important to remember that you're selling something, at the end of the day. If you're going to try your hardest to make it seem otherwise, it's only going to make your audience unreactive to what you have to say.

Keep Posts Short & Specific

The one key element of Facebook marketing is to keep your customer's attention – if your customer sees posts that are too long, or if your all your posts are videos, they're not going to engage a lot.

Be direct with your audience and tell them what you're selling, while trying to connect with them at the same time. Most brands tend to have far more success with shorter posts than they do with huge advertising campaigns.

If you do decide to make longer posts, remember to add pictures and paragraphs. This will at least make your audience interested enough to continue reading.

Facebook Strategies

When it comes to setting up a killer page on Facebook, it is important to make it as interesting for your audience as you can. You must put in the effort to make it look as professional as possible, as well, to help your audience connect with it more effectively.

Here are some strategies that you can employ to make your Facebook page entertaining for your audience:

Personality

It is important for you to add a certain amount of personality to your Facebook page. People should be drawn in by it and feel the urge to like or comment on your content. If you settle for something mediocre, then it will not work in your favor. A good idea is to hire professionals who are good at molding pages and making them interesting for the audience. Instruct them to review your target audience and prepare an analysis of their general characteristics. Doing so helps in preparing a fitting schedule that will make your page popular. You can also look at the strategies that other companies are employing and come up with a plan that is in keeping with the same. However, it is best to maintain a little originality and remain true to your company's policies.

It pays to have a good sense of who you are and what your company stands for. If you remain confused, this will work against you. It is best to develop an image that you would like to portray and then pursue the same. Remember that things can look like one thing in your mind and another on paper. So it is best to create a page and ensure it looks exactly like you planned it.

Consistency

Remember that consistency is key. You have to be consistent with your posts, and they should be coherent. Your Facebook page should be a slice of your store and the products you sell there. Don't make it too different, as this can confuse your customers. If you have a team working for you, instruct them to post content at regular intervals and not keep the audience waiting. A good trick is to know when people prefer to see an update come their way and schedule your content to publish during those times. But don't make it boring, as you want to keep your audience engaged. Again, you can look at a successful company's strategy and come up with a posting schedule that suits your own business. As mentioned earlier, it is best to aim for the early evening slot, as that's when most people are active online.

Frequency

When it comes to maintaining an online profile for your company, it is extremely important to update often. You must try to schedule new posts at regular intervals so people know what to expect and when to expect them. A golden rule is to post in the evenings, as that is when most people expect new content. Try to increase the frequency of the posts as and when the company grows. Some companies prefer to post new posts thrice a day, as that helps in keeping the audience glued. But it is important not to get carried away and post too many things all at once. You cannot overload the audience with too much information, as it will end up confusing them. Keep the information relevant and coherent. You can always do a short trial and error to see what is working for you and what isn't. For example, you can ask your audience how often they would like to receive an email from you. If they are happy with the frequency, you can maintain it, or change it according to their preferences.

Business Goals

It is quite important to be in sync with your business goals and update your page from time to time by keeping in mind your main motivations. Your page should be a thorough representation of your company speaking to your ambitions and portraying your true intentions. It pays to incorporate a little of your company's policies in every new post.

Converting your Profile to a Business Page

If you already have a Facebook profile and wish to convert it into a page without creating a separate one, you can do so easily. Here are some simple instructions:

At the top right-hand corner of your Facebook profile, you will find a drop-down button. Under that, you will find "manage pages", which gives you the option to "create a page." Click here, and you will be able to add a page to your current profile. There, you will be able to automatically convert your current profile into a page.

You can also merge your profile with your page. Click settings and download a copy of your Facebook page, then select the profile to page migration option. Remember, once it is merged, you won't be able to retrieve your profile. You have to make up your mind before making the transition. To merge your business page, go to settings, choose the general tab, and select either the merge pages and merge duplicate pages, then choose the pages that you want to merge. But remember, the two pages have to be identical — including same exact address and information — otherwise, they will not merge into one.

It is easier to create a brand-new page dedicated to your company. However, you will have to fill in all the different details from scratch.

Merchandize

It is a good idea to start with the merchandise. This includes offering exclusive goods that are not available at the store. For example, you can offer a new product that people can only buy through your Facebook page or website and not at the store. Alternately, you can offer a customized product that is exclusively available online. Say, for example, you offer to customize a product to the customer's liking by changing the color scheme or encrypting a message, etc. You can also offer a product in a color scheme or pattern that is different from whatever is available in the store. Make it obvious by posting appropriate announcements and tell your customers they are online exclusives. You can also tell the people in your store to check it out online in order to direct their attention to your Facebook page.

Offers

You can run exclusive online offers, as well. These can include schemes such as buy one get one free, or get a complimentary gift, etc. Such offers are sure to generate interest and enhance your page's value. Again, it is important to advertise, so people are made aware of the offer. You can send out emails detailing the same and tell people about the offers you have made available to your online audience. You can also advertise it in your store or hand out flyers to people, encouraging them to visit your Facebook page.

Rewards

You can reward people who bring in a specific number of likes, too. This works well as people will be prompted to bring in more and more potential new customers to like your page. The reward needs to be a little appealing in order to capture your audience's interest. You can offer coupons, free merchandise, or specially-designed merchandise. All of these will prove to be quite appealing and help lure in more people to like your page. You can make an announcement on the page as well as on your other social media accounts. You can also mention it on your website and inform the people who visit your physical store.

Discount coupons

You can offer discount coupons and discounts to your customers. These coupons will allow them to pay a lower amount for the products and services that you have on offer in your store. They will be able to avail these coupons only on the Facebook page. Again, you must announce it on all your social media accounts, such as Twitter and Instagram, to inform people.

Contests

Contests are a fun way to get people to visit your page. These help people get involved in an exciting way. The contest should be related to the products or services that you offer, like adding a tagline or completing a phrase or posting pictures of the products. You can announce the contest on your Facebook page, and ensure that you also announce a good prize that will excite people enough to partake in the contest. Setting a short deadline is a must, as you will have the chance to increase your page views in a short period of time.

Events

You can also announce events, where people can meet up and get to know each other better. Such events will also help you know your own audience. You can organize food and drinks, as well.

Events can help you out a lot if they are done correctly. All you have to do is create an interesting event, invite as many people as you can, and spread awareness with the help of your page. The benefit from this is that you don't have to spend a ton of money sponsoring events organized by other people — a lot of people sponsor local events to get name recognition.

However, you can use Facebook to gain name recognition without spending a lot of money through events. Events can become very well-known if they are publicized in the right way. First, you'll need to identify the kind of event that your target audience would be interested in. Once you have done that, start inviting people and spread the word about the event.

Say you are a local bakery who wants name recognition in your locality. Start by thinking of a creative event you can use to publicize your business while also giving your customers a fun time. Create a related event on Facebook and start inviting people that you know are in your area; use your contacts as well as your Facebook page. Use the event to promote your company, and keep publicizing your bakery so that your small business gets name recognition.

This is just the start — by spending a little more money, you can create events that will attract thousands of people. Start slowly with events that won't require a significant investment, and once you see that the events are helping streamline revenue, you can start expanding to bigger events to get even more name recognition.

These are just some of the different offers you can run online, and are not limited to just these. You can modify them all to suit your company's policies.

Reasons Why You Should Use Facebook Advertising

You have seen how you can use Facebook for your business, now let's look at the reasons why you should use Facebook for advertising.

1. Facebook advertising is extremely effective. Because of how many people are on Facebook, it's hard to ignore that Facebook is a major part of everyone's life. In fact, Facebook is considered to be one of the top advertising channels online because digital ads make up 51% of total advertising in the United States.

2. Simple set up and fast results. Setting up a Facebook campaign is going to take very little time and will provide you with excellent results. Digital advertising produces terrific ROI and will be extremely fast when you assign the best campaign strategy with the best product that you have to offer. Facebook has the tools to help you drive traffic to your website and even allows you to boost single posts.

3. You can reach the perfect audience. You have already seen how you can design the perfect clientele that will help you when it comes to targeting the right demographic. It's also going to make your advertising more successful.

4. Facebook campaigns are customizable. You'll be able to create the perfect ad experience because it will only be seen by your specified audience choice. All of this is made possible because of the different ad formats that Facebook provides you when you create your ad campaigns.

5. Facebook adds new features every month. Because of how adaptive Facebook is your ads will constantly evolve to reach the perfect audience.

6. You can set your own budget on Facebook which is going to allow you to advertise for as little as $1. Even though this is a small budget, your campaign is still going to reach a lot of people.

7. You can easily track your performance and ROI with the analytic tools that Facebook provides such as your ad manager.

8. You'll get an edge over your competitors because not everyone is using Facebook, or they are not using it properly. therefore, you're going to gain an advantage over your competition. So, exploit it while you can!

9. Facebook is compelling with regards to push going back and forth leads down the pipeline. This strategy will work for any marketer that is trying to target their clients that have already visited your website which means that they are

most likely going to be attracted to your business on some level.

10. Facebook makes it easy for you to find new leads. As you saw earlier, you'll have the tools with Facebook business manager that will let you look at people who are interested in specific hobbies or certain pages that will lead you to more people who could be interested in your business but have yet to hear about you.

Facebook Pixel

So, what is Facebook Pixel? A lot of people tend to forget about Facebook Pixel because the internet is filled with cookies. Cookies will track the movements of your website visitors. In the end, Pixels are just the same as cookies.

Facebook Pixel Functions

Pixels have multiple actions that will aid you while you're creating your marketing campaigns.

1. Track conversions: Conversions will be any action that your visitors complete. Facebook Pixel is able to keep track of 9 different types of conversions that will be available to you in order for you to improve your conversion rate and targeting. Take for example, you're running a campaign that costs $1 per click and get up to 500 clicks. Pixel is going to be able to tell you exactly how many people clicked on the ad and how it's actually converted.

2. Optimize ads for conversions: One of the biggest differences between Google Analytics and Facebook Pixel will be how Facebook uses the information collected by Pixel. Instead of just

showing you what is seen, Facebook will collect the data and then target people who are similar to those that are already being converted. Therefore, by optimizing your targeting which will help to improve your chances for success.

3. Retargeting ads: Online, retargeting will be when you send ads to those that have already shown an interest in your site or have interacted with you before. Facebook's Pixels will allow you to retarget people who have performed a specific action on your website.

Take for instance, if you visit an airline website to search for trips, you'll notice that once you leave the site, there will be more ads that are related to traveling. You're not imagining this. You're being targeted so they can get you to spend money on their site.

Most marketers know that retargeting customers will be easier to convert because they have already visited your site. That means that they are more likely to become a normal customer.

Creating a Facebook Pixel

Facebook Pixel can sound scary, but it's a lot easier to do than you think. Here we will go through the steps to creating a Facebook Pixel.

1. Enter your ad account and select the menu choice. From this point you should go to "all tools" which is going to expand the menu. You'll then click on "Pixcl" which can be found under measure and report.

2. Facebook will then prompt you to create your own Pixel.

3. The only thing that you're going to need to do is provide a name for your Pixel. The name is not going to be public therefore you can name it something that is logical to you.

4. You'll be required to accept the terms of conditions.

5. Now you'll click on the option that will give you a new menu. When adding Pixel to your website, a lot of people decide to manually install it, or you can email the instructions to a developer if that is easier for you.

6. Last, you'll copy the code that is provided and add it to your website.

If this is the case, you'll want to use the integration or tag manager option rather than manually install the code yourself one.

From there you're going to click on the Shopify icon and then copy the integration code that is provided.

Adding Pixel to WordPress or Shopify
There are a couple of different methods that can be used in order to add Pixel to your website.

1. Direct upload to WordPress. Follow these simple steps in order to install Pixel.

x. Go to your WordPress dashboard and click on the left menu. From there you'll click on appearance and editor.

y. file. On the right-hand side you'll move to theme files, you'll scroll down till you see the theme header or header.php. You're now going to be able to edit your WordPress theme's header

z. Scroll down until you can see the closing head tag.

aa. Add in a few blank lines between the closing head tag and any code before it. Now you'll insert the Pixel code to the new blank lines.

bb. Save your file and upload it with an FTP program.

Note: When you decide to change your theme, you'll have to go through this process again because Pixel will be removed from the theme changes.

2. Through a WordPress plugin. This is recommended when you're inserting headers and footers. But there are a variety of plugins that you can use if you want.

cc. From the left menu, choose plugins and add new.

dd. Use your search on the lower right side in order to find the plugin you want to use.

ee. Install and activate the header and footer plugin to your website.

ff. Now move back to your menu and choose settings before clicking on insert headers and footers.

gg. open your plugin and search for scripts in header before pasting the Pixel code in the proper box.

hh. Save and refresh your page.

One of the best benefits when it comes to this plugin is that when you change themes, your Pixel is still going to be on your website.

Note: If you're using Pixel on one website, you can install the Facebook Pixel helper which is located on Chrome. This is going to allow you to see any events that are happening in real time.

    3. Shopify direct upload. This method should only be utilized if you feel comfortable updating your site's theme.

ii. Got Shopify and click on the online store.

jj. On your new menu you'll click on themes.

kk. In the themes section you'll click on actions and then click on edit code.

ll. Under the layout folder you'll need to click on the theme that you're currently using.

mm. Scroll down until you see the closing head tag.

nn. Make sure you add in a few lines before the head tag and any code that comes before it. You'll then enter your Pixel code into these blank lines.

oo. Click save.

    4. Shopify integration. Since some people are not comfortable when it comes to editing code, Shopify has created a simpler method so you don't have to mess with any of the code.

pp. Go to Shopify and click on the online store off the left-hand side menu.

qq.   In your new menu, select preferences.

rr.   ON this new page, move down until you see a box that asks you about your Pixel id.

ss.   Paste your Pixel id into the box.

tt.   Save your new changes.

Installing and using Pixel may end up being the most effective marketing strategy that you'll decide to use. It's only going to be a few steps that you have to follow in order to have access to powerful analytics on your website.

Creating High-Quality Facebook Content for Your Audience

If you want to keep increasing the number of visitors on your Facebook page or group, you need to be consistent with the content that you offer. You will gain their interest and promote engagement if you always provide high-quality content.

Here are some steps you can follow to create noteworthy Facebook posts for your audience.

Change Up the Content You Upload

Don't make the content you publish appear monotonous. It's not every time your audience will be interested in reading a long post. Sometimes, having a photo gallery to scroll through is beneficial as well. You should create a balance between the following types of contents:

Press Releases

These should contain information regarding changes in your business policies, service improvements, and general updates.

Blog Posts

Articles should provide details that will benefit your customers or describe anything new that goes on with the business.

Videos

They may consist of how-to, motivational, and other types of beneficial videos.

Photos

You can upload pictures of your products, office building, workers, or events.

Let Your Fans Contribute to the Wall
When you want to attract a specific audience, the Facebook page should become your fan page. It will be incomplete if your visitors don't have the option of posting directly on your wall. To promote engagement with your customers and fans, therefore, make sure to have this feature enabled. If you are unsure how to do that, you may check your settings.

Always Captivate Your Audience
The quality or relevance of your content will not matter if your presentation is boring. You must showcase it in a way that interests your audience.

If your business is in the gaming sector, for instance, your viewers will stop going through posts, considering they only tell them how to clean their consoles or maintain their accessories. Why don't you have a top ten review or pick the best games you have played instead? You don't have to be an expert at it; you can share your opinions on the games that you wish to recommend.

Professionalism may not be the best option when running a business on Facebook. A lot of times, you will need to be able to interact at the same level as your target audience. This can show them how important they are to you.

Leave a Question After Each Post to Promote Interaction

Everyone wants the post they see to feel personal. Your visitors will not feel the need to comment on it if there is no question to prompt a response from them.

To entice people to interact and leave a comment on your page, you should add questions after every post. A call to action is another alternative to promote engagement on the page as well.

Now, depending on what your post covers, there are numerous questions you may ask. If you uploaded a video on "tips for smoother skin," for instance, you can encourage your viewers to comment about their personal experience with the tips or share other suggestions on how to smoothen the skin. Remember: a good question is all you need to start an excellent conversation with potential consumers.

Align Your Content with Your Audience's Interests

It is easy to get comfortable with posting content that only relates to your business. After all, you are running your brand's page or group. However, you should also provide information that will be beneficial to your customers.

If you sell athletic shoes, for example, then you are sure that most - if not all - of your consumers focus on fitness. Sharing some videos with excellent workout tips, therefore, may be appreciable for them. If customers know that they can rely on you to get information, it can help to solidify your relationship.

Don't Oversaturate the News Feed

When you want a large number of people to notice your page, you may consider uploading a lot of posts to get their attention. If you are already halfway through this door, it is advisable for you to step out.

The reason is that many Facebook users will block you quickly if their newsfeed is getting filled up with your posts alone. You are not giving them any room to view feeds from their friends and family on the platform.

If you want your content to get more attention, you should have a regular day and time when you upload them. If you stay consistent with the quality of the posts, your audience will look forward to the days when you will be publishing them.

Tailor Your Posts to Suit the Facebook Platform

With so many social media platforms available, each one has some aspects that make them unique. Say, on Twitter, the '#' and '@' are the symbols that appear frequently. While most Twitter users understand what they represent, a lot of Facebook users may not. Hence, you are lifting one of your posts off Twitter, it is necessary to edit the post to suit Facebook's standard. You don't want to cause a misunderstanding between you and your audience, after all.

Promote Creativity Through Your Contests

Since fan pages commonly host contests, you need to be creative to make yours stand out. The online competitions you hold may come with a video, photo or essay entry. To promote creativity, you can ask your customers to come up with costume, logo or art designs, as well as articles that you may post on your blog or website.

If a participant submits an entry, remember to tag your customers when uploading it on your page. By doing so, the post will show up on their wall and become visible to their friends and followers. It is an easy way to reach more Facebook users.

Don't Get Carried Away by Hosting Contests
When building a great fan page, hosting contests play a vital role in your success. Any competition you host should excite your audience and turn into a fun activity for the participants. Nevertheless, keep in mind that their effectiveness will dwindle if you host them too often.

A good strategy to use when scheduling contests is to choose dates close to an upcoming event. Having an Easter egg hunt during the Easter season, for instance, will help get them into the Easter mood.

Choose One Topic for a Month
Having a unique topic to cover in a month is a great way to keep your audience interested. In addition to the posts that you will upload on your page, you also need to add links to other sites where your viewers can get more information about the topic.

If all your content revolve around a single subject, your viewers will quickly lose interest in them. Besides, you are likely to run out of exciting things to talk about by doing so. When you provide various topics, though, you can expand your target audience.

Get a handle on success today. Start publishing high-quality content that will captivate and engage your audience as much as possible.

Understanding the Facebook Group

Creating Facebook Group

The process of creating a Facebook group is quite simple. Since you already have a personal profile, you can create the group using the same account. The first step is to view the options in the drop-down menu on the top right corner of the Facebook page. You will find the "Create Group" tab there along with the logout and activity log buttons.

The next step is to decide on a name for the group that you are creating. It is essential for it to be similar to that of your existing business if it is in relation to that. By going with this option, your customers from another platform can find you with ease.

Then, you have to invite people to become members of the group. There are different means of doing so.

The first option is to find the individuals you want to find on Facebook and then send an invite to these users. The interested ones will join the group by accepting the invitation. Another option is to forward a group invite to the email address of the users. Getting the latter information should not be an issue since it is standard for most businesses. You can invite members at any time since you will be running the group as an administrator.

After completing the steps above, your next task is to pick the group type.

- Secret groups
- Closed groups
- Public groups

A secret group is not visible to other Facebook users. It is not possible to find it if you are not a member. The things posted on this group are exclusive as well.

The closed group is quite similar to the secret group. Unlike the secret groups, all Facebook users can search for the community and view details of the members. Only the content posted on the group remains private.

The last and most common type you will find is the public group. It refers to online communities that do not require someone to become a member before viewing the posts there.

Selecting a Group Icon

Another area to consider when creating the group is choosing a group icon. The icon will appear in different ways at the side of the group name. It is necessary to make your group stand out since it appears along with the group name in a search result.

Chapter 9 Instagram Marketing

Instagram Contents

As stated earlier, Instagram is a platform that works by visuals posts. Everything shared are either photos, graphics or videos. Because of this, very many people find it hard to create contents; many don't even know how to post or whether a posting is allowed. Those that know these are confused on what sort of content should be on Instagram. In this section, you will be taken through the parts of the content, types of contents and processes of creating content on Instagram. Attention is paid keenly to direct you through crafting perfect posts.

Because of the nature of the platform, visuals and branded storytelling are the keys of contents used. To engage your followers as a business-oriented person, telling a story about your product and services is the key to being the best seller. Posting pictures that are 'meaningless' will never add anything to your account. On Instagram, create a story that will be of great impact to your followers and any potential ones. The best thing to do is to put your gaze on your followers. You must, with utmost clarity, put them into consideration because they are the one to be engaged. Be adroit in your post to ensure entertainment and genuine contents. Be skillful in the way you arrange your photos. While uploading the photos, show them the nature of people in support of your business, the type of person you are, the muse of your story, and lots more. Don't take the time of your audience; make the story succinct and exclusive to Instagram news only. Be dynamic in the chronological arrangement of the stories. To ensure uniqueness of your profile, make sure you are updated on the latest trends on the platform. These trends could be news or hashtags, write on them and use them as well. Devise a way of connecting your interesting contents in such a way that your followers will have to stay on your profile to get the full story. Get the interaction with them interesting; they will surely look up for more. There are some basic things to consider while constructing a good Instagram content. These, according to Martins, are:

The Right time

You have to skillfully detect the right time to post your story based on your targeted audience. You must be up-to-date on their personal activities. Note that on your newsfeed, the most recent posts receive more attention which is why your post must be timely. You must key into an opportunity such as this. According to Martin "if your viral page is aimed at students who are online in the morning, then you should post in this period." This means the free time which your targeted audience is likely to be free to check their Instagram should be considered before posting. He gave another example that if you have 9-to5-jobbers as a target group, then you should write more posts after work. These people will have free time randomly; by this, you must post in their timing too. He, however, gave a recommendation which is not 'convenient test' as generally 7-9 clock (breakfast), 11-14 clock (lunch) and 17 to 20 clock (after work). The best interaction on Instagram was also given as 17-18 clock. The time frame of your location should not affect your audience consideration. Although most times, you and your followers are in the same meridian.

The Picture

Instagram can also be referred to as an electronic photo album. This is because it contains much of them. The pictures to be posted must be very attractive. Consider editing your photos before uploading them. Make sure the post is dynamic with different types of things such as comedy videos, photos and all. Try to upload pictures that are showing the practical time people are consuming your product. Research has it that many people consider photos from real life scenes of the product as the authenticity of the product. High-quality photos are recommended; make sure you don't post low-quality photos and videos. Be dynamic in the selection and arrangement of the pictures. Make sure you include a brand of your company on a photo that is not really related. Don't let your followers have bad impressions about you. If you make necklaces, consider using your friends as part of the models and then take their pictures for onward uploads on to your account. Take pictures of people that have worn the necklace to events such as weddings to authenticate it. Being outstanding should be your goal by creating compelling contents that entertain people. The type of pictures you will post for children will be different from the adults'. You must do all your best to get their target at different times as well. You should catch their attention at once sometimes too. The arrangement of your pictures also matters. The recommended arrangement is the grid formula. With a grid, you have the opportunity to arrange your pictures chronologically to explain the story you are telling. Apart from this, followers can quickly trace the story effortlessly. The posts must be able to hold anyone that runs across the posts; they must locate your account and follow.

The Text

Even though Instagram is basically visual, texts could be added to it sometimes too. Most times, these texts should be one that will require the action of the followers. The texts should vary between lengthy words and short ones. The place your company is located will be an additional text for you in cases you don't know the text to use. The aim is to engage your followers. Your text must be relevant to your pictures and most times should be one or two words. When you include your location, the post will be expanded to reach more audience thereby popularizing the account –this is your goal. Make sure the text is proofread, don't spoil the mind of the people that are already interested in you. Text can be a statement on the images uploaded as well. With this, if you are uploading pictures that are not a direct replica of your product, many of your followers will understand vividly.

Best steps to creating audience-centered contents

Having a business account requires the consistent engagement of your audience. This makes good contents an unavoidable thing to be included in your profile. You can consider the following tricks given by Instagram influencer Christina Galbato when creating a laudable content:

Use ready-made templates tools

When you want to create contents on Instagram and wonder how to create a pattern for them or perhaps stumbled on a great profile with nice and cool contents, and you want to create, template tools is what top Instagram influencers used. There are lots of tools Canva, Venngage and Adobe with great Spark posts. These tools will craft an outstanding content that titillates the eyes and leave the mind wondering what sort the pictures is. You don't need to stress yourself, search for any of these tools, insert your pictures and you will be wowed by the outcome. It has trial sections, and you can equally choose manually that template you love.

- ❖ *Research and Use High-quality stock images*

That you will need lots of images is a fact. On the contrary, stock images could be awkward on your news-feed. Be extremely careful while using it most especially with templates. Everyone needs varying images to be created as contents, visit Stocksnap.io or Un-splash for free nice images. If you are buoyant enough, you could log onto Stocksy for images with high quality, different niche pictures, etc. Stocksy provides the greatest images because it is paid for and the developers want it to be worth it. Bear in mind that the standard pixel for images to be uploaded as content on Instagram is 1080p X 1080p to avoid automatic image resolutions. Stock images are always great and nice because the sites where they are found were actually developed to meet the criteria of social platforms such as Instagram.

Vary your content's format

Dynamism is the way forward in having a good followers' turn up on your content. You can't be deaf to the reaction of the followers when creating your contents. You could create a short video, say of 1-minute duration, explaining your product or showing the practical usage of your product. Don't bore your viewers with just a single type of pictures; it could be extremely boring really. A good Instagram profile will house varying contents. The distinction in the contents is only in their format. Take your time to create GIF contents as well. You could have a picture, GIF and short video and their permutation as well. This is what your audience is expecting, give them. Though Instagram takes both GIF and Videos as the same thing, GIF is always shorter but interactive. Lots of people expect it as well. Stuff your contents with a variety of formats.

Search for brands within your niche and repost them

Perhaps creating contents yourself is barely possible because of time constraints. Don't worry; there is a way out of the tunnel. You can, with the consent of the writer, report a post within your niche from another content writer. Example of posts you could repost are those posts from fast-growing Instagram users. They must be of interest to your audience though. However, on Instagram, there are special steps to go through in order to make reposting official –reposting without proper consultation could lead to offense. Follow the steps below:

1. Follow hashtags and accounts to find out quality content

In order to validate your reposting, ensure that you have a similar audience and brand. Make the person you want repost his/her content is not a direct competitor to you. Make sure you have proper thinking on the content as well. You must follow the person in order to be updated on the posts of the person. To save the contents you would love to repost, try to create a collection for easy access. Searching for related contents through hashtag is also a legal way.

2. Contact the user for permission to repost

Before asking for permission, make sure you let the writer know they are doing a great job with proper credit and that your audience will be interested in the same post. To ask for permission, send the writer a DM through the arrow beneath the picture. Using the arrow has proven most efficient way, according to the report, of sending a direct message to account users.

3. Share the picture on your news feed

You can now share the picture to your feed once the permission has been granted. You must make sure proper credit is given to the source of the post anyway.

4. Save the Photo from Instagram or share directly through the repost feature

There are two ways of reposting on Instagram: saving from Instagram and reposting directly. For the first one, you will need to find the picture, click on the photo, double click it, view page source, type jpg there, copy the URL of the first option, open a new browser, paste it there, right click and save the picture. On the second option, copy the URL of the post you like and click on "repost" and it will automatically repost it. Note that the watermark is maintained when you use the second option. The first looks complex likewise, try to accompany the process given with required practical.

Create a UGC Campaign

The acronym UGC means 'User Generated Content.' It is used as content created by your followers. You could be the initiator, and they could post within your niche. This is also an activity similar to reposting of contents. User-generated content is typically contents crafted by any product user on their products without encouragement from anyone. These are contents solicited by you from your followers, though most times with incentives to encourage them. You can involve your followers in different ways: selling your product at a discount rate, conducting a competition on creating a post on your brand, etc. Instagram has suggested that you announce your hashtag even on other platforms especially the part of the incentives. Be strategic and dynamic in your request for contents from your audience. Without dynamism in your request, your feed will always be the same thing which will bore your audience. If you stipulate too many rules are guiding the kind of post you want, you might end up with no post as many people might be afraid they won't be considered. Relying too much on your followers is not a good idea as well. Make sure their posts are just supplementary and not the main thing. Proof to them you can actually create your content yourself and create a feeling that their support is a means to encourage them only.

Do influencer collaboration

One fantastic thing to do to create a good audience-centered profile is to work with other great brand promoters too. This will get you new followers, great feed and many other things enjoyed by the person you collaborated with. You must ensure the collaboration is with someone within your own niche to avoid exploitation and misunderstanding. Worry less on how to contact top influencers as many of them have a contact in their bio basically for collaboration inquiries purpose.

You have learned how to create good content for your brand and business. However, note that whatever means you are using to get your contents, designing will surely be done by you. Because of this, you will need to learn basic tricks used by top influencers to design their contents. These tricks are:

✓   *Stating a precise focal point*
While uploading your pictures and creating your format, make sure your photo has focus. The focus of photos means the center where you want your viewers to pay their attention only. If you create a picture with lots of images on, you might lose the focus, affecting its effect on the viewers. Therefore, put a single image with many other things, if need be, pointing only to the central idea of the photo.

✓   *Adhere to the rule of thirds*
The rule of thirds, found in photography, is all about arranging your interesting features along with a 9-grid picture intersection. This rule is a classic rule and executed by 9-grid photo imagination. Make sure that in uploading many pictures on your profile, you must adhere strictly to this rule –it is the secret of the top influencers. With amazing third rule obedience, you will adjust your grid to one-third of the picture you wish to upload as well.

✓   *Create and apply white space and borders*
Creating space and borders around your photos gives it a compelling look, and the audience will always want to gaze more. To avoid jam-packed uploads, ensure that you maintain some space between your third rule and focal point picture. Make sure you add this effect to all your posts, and you will experience rapid growth of followers.

✓   *Rapt attention should be to Contrast and balance*
Give your picture a good contrast while uploading. The contrast of your picture ranges over its color, light, shape, fonts, white space and border, and lots more. To ensure you have a perfect contrast setting, you could play around the various types of it on your Instagram app. Contrast is an important part of content designed to highly engage your audience. Many people are fascinated by the enhancement of

a given picture even before focusing on the content itself. Contrast is like a finishing effect that 'crowns' your effort in content design. This is the last stage of content design, make sure it counts, and you will be amazed by the number of turn out your account will experience.

Using Instagram Live

Why Use Instagram Live for Business?

Just like you would use stories, it is important to use Instagram Live for your business. Not only can it be a great channel for connecting with your audience and increasing followers, but also going after business goals and generating leads. It can also help you get discovered better on Instagram.

Just like Instagram stories, making interesting Instagram Live videos can help you show up on the explore page that can make it easier to find you. It will be easier to broadcast your message and connect better with your audiences.

Instagram Live can be quite flexible as you get to decide what to broadcast and offer workshops, and answer questions etc.

You can make it fun and engaging for your audience to hold their attention.

How to Use Instagram Live for Business

Just like stories, Instagram Live can be used as an easy tool to broadcast a live video. Here are some things to keep in mind:

Viewers

You get to choose who to broadcast live to. You do not have to do it for all, and select only a few to broadcast to. You can choose to hide it from specific accounts by selecting the "Hide Story From" option.

Moderating Comments

As you know, when you go live, you allow people to comment on your video and you will not have control over what they say. If you wish to avoid any language that is inappropriate, then it is best to go to the settings and find "Comments" and go to "Hide Inappropriate Comments" and turn it from off to on. You can add custom keywords that you wish to appear in the comments.

Setting up a Live Broadcast

- Start by swiping right on the home screen or the camera icon on the top left to access the camera.

- Choose the "Live" camera option and "Start Live Video" option. If your notifications are off, then your audience might not be notified when you go live so make sure you switch on notifications.

- The number of people viewing will appear on the top and their comments at the bottom.

- Once done, touch the "End" button in the top right corner and "End Live Video."

Instagram Ads and Ad Budget

When it comes to creating ads for Instagram, it is important to use the right tools to create appealing ads. Here are some types of ads you can choose to make for your products:

Photo Ads

Single image ads help to create about six ads that contain an image each.

- To create them, start by choosing the images you wish to use in the ads.

- Go through the library and upload pictures or choose free stock images.

- Add the caption you would want to use for the ad in the text field.

- The caption can be 300 characters long with the third line having ellipsis that will make the audience click on expand to view it fully.

- It is ideal to choose 125 characters for ads as otherwise it can be burdening.

- You can add a website link or a URL.

- You do not have to fill out all the fields such as the display link, headline, link description etc.

- Go to advanced options to change pixels or advanced tracking.

Video Ads

Single video ads are comprised of a video or a gif.

- To create them, go to the video thumbnail and add a video from your gallery or shoot one.

- Upload one that runs for 15 seconds for best results.

- If you wish to caption the video, then use an SRT file.

- It is best to add captions using 125 characters just as in the case of photo ads. Again, limit it to 125 characters.

Slideshow Ads

Slideshow ads are nothing but video ads that play on loop and can have 10 images with music supplementing it.

- To create them, go to the library and create a slideshow using the creator.

- Add the images and then arrange them to your liking and adjust the settings. Add in music if you like by choosing the icon on the top right.

Carousel Ads

Carousel ads are made up of images and videos.

- To make them, create cards for the ads. You can add up to 10 cards at a time.

- Add in headline or caption or text to each of the cards.

- You can choose to leave the description empty or add a URL.

- Add lead forms as it makes for an important step of the process.

- Regardless of the ad format you choose, create your lead form.

- If you already have one, then you can use the same or make a new one for the ads.

- If you wish to make one, then the fields to fill out includes the welcome screen, headline, image, layout, button text, questions, privacy policy, and thank you screen etc.

- A website link can also be added.

- Once done, click on the finish button.

- Once you click on it, you will not be able to edit it.

How Much Does it Cost?

How much the ads will cost will depend on the budget you set for it and whether you wish to use the manual or automatic bidding system.

As per marketing experts, running your ads on Instagram will be almost twice as cost-effective as running them on other social media platforms such as Facebook.

Although it is difficult to assess how much an ad can cost, it is safe to assume that the ad can be around $5. This is half of what it takes to come up with Facebook ads that can be around $10.

Don't worry about your budget going bust, as you will hardly ever over-shoot it when making Instagram ads.

Make sure you are well aware of what will be going into making the ads to be able to come up with an effective budget for it.

Instagram Analytics

Analytics play a very important role when it comes to understanding the effectiveness of the content that is being sent out. It helps the company understand the reach and the engagement. It is therefore important to understand the different performance indicators that can help companies know the effectiveness of their ad campaigns being carried out on Instagram.

Reach

Reach refers to the number of people who can view the content that has been posted on the brand's page. This content has to be relevant and great for it to be popular on the platform's search tab in order to reach a bigger audience.

If you go by benchmarks, then it will be easy to improve the content that is being sent out. It helps to build content that appeal to the audience and increases brand value. If the profile has a lot of views, it will be easy to draw in more people to follow the page and increase the product's reach.

Engagement

Customer engagement is an important part of using Instagram as a means to connect with the audience. It can be measured through the 'likes' and comments that have been posted for a picture. The comments usually include the brand's hashtag, which will help to understand the activity taking place. It is possible to track down a lot of information, such as the filters that are popular, the content that is selling best, and styles that are a hit etc. It will be best to carry out a trial and error to understand what is working well for your audience and use it as a benchmark to improve the content that is being put out on your page.

Here is a summary of what analytics can do for you:

- Reach out to more customers and keep them engaged.
- Measure the key performance indicators.
- Create a benchmark for customers.
- Collect and understand the data.
- Make changes and improvements in the posts with the data that is connected.

Chapter 10 YouTube Marketing

Live Streaming on YouTube

Like Facebook, YouTube offers live streaming functions. This allows you to display things in real time to anyone around the world. It offers a fun layout where you can highlight anything unique or of value to you.

Over the years YouTube has been used to stream various events live. It has streamed concerts, governmental meetings, conferences, sporting events, and much more. The audiences for these events can be impressive as well. For instance, in 2012 nearly eight million people went on YouTube to watch Felix Baumgartner jump out of an aircraft more than 20 miles above the earth's surface.

Fortunately, you don't have to be like Baumgartner and jump from the edge of the planet's atmosphere just to be noticed on YouTube. You just have to produce a smart video conference or other event to interact with people and share anything you want with them.

Live streaming works best when you want to talk with potential customers or wish to go to some special event, and share it online. Several steps must be used when getting a live stream ready.

Use the Stream Now Option
You can start streaming live by using the Stream Now option on your YouTube account. This works when you have an appropriate encoder. The Stream Now selector lets you get onto a streaming session on YouTube right away. Use this to send content at any time; YouTube will automatically start a stream when you get ready and end it when you finish.

1. Go to the Creator Studio and then the Live Streaming section.

2. *Set up your encoder.*

An encoder is a device or software program that compresses your audio and video into a setup that YouTube can support. You can download one of various encoders for your use including Webcam, Mobile Live, Air-Server, Sling-Studio, and Gameshow, among many others.

3. Enter a title and description for the video.

4. Add a thumbnail to your stream. This will let people know what your stream is about.

5. *Prepare a schedule for when the stream begins. It is recommended to let people know when you will stream ahead of time.*

6. Set your privacy setting.

You can make your live stream public or unlisted. Or a private session only available to subscribers, or people who enter with a password. If you wish to make it private, you will be prompted to enter a password for access or to use an option to let subscribers in.

7. Choose the latency option. High-quality latency is the best viewing quality; low-quality latency is best for real-time use.

8. If you only have the rights to the live content, click on the box to archive your stream as unlisted when finished.

Using the Events Option

You can also stream on YouTube through the Events option. The Events choice lets you plan your YouTube stream as a special occasion ahead of time.

1. Go to the Live Streaming section of the Creator Studio.

2. *Click the Events section and then the New Live Event option.*

3. Enter the basic points of the event.

The critical features to list include the title and description of the event, when it starts and ends, plus any tags you want to incorporate.

4. Set the privacy option. Use Public for events that appear on your channel.

5. *Select the Quick option. This will get the event supported through YouTube Live, the official live streaming support system used by YouTube.*

6. Make sure the item you use for recording yourself is accessible during the event.

Using Live Chat

The Live Chat feature on YouTube lets you interact with others during a live streaming event. This lets you talk to people online about anything happening in your stream.

The chat box appears on the right-hand side of your video player. It is visible when the video recording process is running.

How to use Live Chat:

1. Use either the Top chat or Live chat display. The Top chat option filters out possible spam messages. The Live chat displays everything.

2. *Assign a moderator for your chat. Click on the three dots near your chat box and enter someone's username to be approved as a moderator.*

Make sure the moderator is also someone within your business. The moderator will review all the things being entered into a live chat. The person should let you know what people are saying.

3. Go to the Community Settings section of the live chat and enter blocked words. Any chat messages that feature certain words will be blocked.

4. Block viewers from your live chat if they become abusive by clicking next to a questionable chat message, going to the writer's YouTube channel, and then clicking on the Block flag from the user's About page.

All the comments left during your chat will be accessible under your live streaming player after the stream ends.

Using Live Metrics

Make sure you read the live analytics or metrics on your streaming video. This gives you information on how many people are watching, how many messages are coming into your video, and how long people have been viewing your video and some other points.

You will not have access to every metric while you are recording. Use the YouTube Analytics feature to identify how your videos are working a few days after the stream ends.

Tips for Live Streaming

There are a few important tips when getting your live streaming experience on YouTube to work for you:

- Let people on YouTube know about your live stream as soon as possible. Tell them when you will stream so they can plan to get onto your page at a certain time.

- Keep a recorded archive of your live event on your hard drive if possible. This ensures you can get the event uploaded onto your page later on.

- Keep the stream looking professional. Use a high-quality camera and microphone to make your stream look its finest. Try to keep the microphone from being visible on the camera; a camera with a built-in microphone might be best.

- You have the option to use a webcam for streaming if needed. A webcam can work to get something ready for recording without having to use an encoder. Make sure the webcam is compatible with YouTube and that It's of good quality.

- Respond to comments during your live stream if possible. Address those who comment by name so people will see that you listen to them and that you have a vested interested in what they say.

- You can always record a live stream while on the go. Make sure the camera and microphone are steady so people can hear and see you properly.

A live stream on YouTube is fun because it offers a unique way to interact with people. Try this option to make your business visible on YouTube. Plan, so you have the best possible event ready.

Using Paid Ads on YouTube Through Google AdWords

The next point for using YouTube for your social media marketing is to utilize the paid ads feature on the site. The TrueView ad system lets you reach people who want to watch your videos on YouTube. Much of this is thanks to how YouTube works with the Google AdWords system.

Google AdWords is a method that lets people get their advertisements to appear higher up on a search. When a person's link is connected to a specific keyword, that link will appear at the top of a search page for that word. Since Google controls YouTube, it should not be difficult to use the marketing system offered here.

For YouTube, AdWords works a little differently. You will spend money on each click someone puts onto your video or every time someone watches your video. The videos and ads you produce will be displayed based on the keywords someone uses to search or the audience you target. The amount you spend depends on how many people click on your ad. A budget can also be set up so that your ad will be removed after you have spent a specified amount.

How Will Your Ad Be Displayed?

There are three ways your ad can be displayed on YouTube through AdWords:

1. It appears as a video that shows up before the desired video.

You can get your ad to play before someone's expected video comes up on YouTube. The user has the option to skip the ad after the first five seconds. You will only have to pay for the video ad when someone watches at least 30 seconds of it. An ad promoting the video will also appear on the top-right corner of the screen after the user watches or skips the video. The skip option makes it all the more important for you to draw the viewer's attention during the first few seconds of the ad.

2. *It could also show up on another website.*

Your video might appear on an outside website through an embedded player. Provided the video is similar in focus to the content on that site. You will pay for the ad when someone watches enough of the video.

3. It can appear on a YouTube search.

As with AdWords on Google, AdWords on YouTube will have your video appear at the top of a search listing. This is when the keyword someone searches for matches up with yours. You will pay money when someone clicks on the link.

Steps to Follow

1. Set up a Google AdWords account at adwords.google.com.

You will have to enter your contact information while also offer details on how you will pay for your ads.

2. *Go to the Campaigns tab and then click on the +Campaign option.*

3. Select the ad you want to work with. Enter the title of your ad, and the proper one should be displayed.

4. Enter the headline you wish to use.

5. *Write a few lines describing the ad.*

6. Determine where the ad will send people.

You can get the ad to redirect people to either your YouTube channel or your home page.

7. Choose the thumbnail you wish to display.

8. Determine the total amount of money you will spend on the ad. This includes how much you will spend for each click and the maximum budget.

The campaign will continue as long as it needs to. You can always remove your ad from the AdWords system on your own later if needed. Don't forget to include a proper payment system for how you will pay for the ads.

You can use a daily budget followed by the maximum cost-per-view. For instance, you could spend up to $0.05 per view for a $10 daily budget. This means your video can appear all day long until 200 people click or watch it and give you qualifying views. The total will reset the next day.

9. *Determine the audience that your video will target.*

Your target audience could be based on:

- Geographic location
- Age
- Gender
- Keyword interests

Make sure you enter the proper parameters based on the video you are promoting. Be specific if you have a particular need for marketing. Remember, your possible reach will shrink when you are more specific. The cost per click or view might also change depending on where you go.

Key Tips

- Always use proper keywords in your video's description.
- Keep the title appealing and friendly so that the user will want to see the ad.
- The content of your video should be relevant to whatever keywords you are incorporating into it.
- Get the viewer's attention as soon as possible. Get it in the first five seconds so the viewer will not skip your ad.
- Be free to tell a longer story if desired. Your video ad can last a few minutes if you want it to.
- Give viewers information on how to act at the end. Ask them to click on a link to your site or to subscribe to your channel.

- Use an end screen during the final ten seconds. The screen should tell the viewer what action to take.

- Be specific when entering in the demographics for your ad. Think about who might be interested in your business when getting this data entered.

What About Bumper Ads?

You can use bumper ads on YouTube if you prefer as well. A bumper ad is a six-second message that lets you create some buzz over what you have. It is not an ad that people can skip either; then again, it is a short commercial. You would have to create a new short ad that can be utilized as a bumper to make this option work.

1. Go to the Campaigns tab of your AdWords account and select the video you want to use. Make sure the ad is short enough to be a bumper.

2. *Go to the Video Ad Formats section and select the Bumper option.*

3. Prepare your budget.

4. Choose where you want to market your ads at.

5. *Save your advertisement.*

Prepare a unique and convenient six-second ad to make your bumper spot attractive and visible. It should be designed with a look that is interesting and special in some way. After all, you only have a limited amount of time to make it attractive.

Creating Ad Groups

Ad groups let you link several video advertisements together. The ads can work with the same budget and target the same people. You can get one ad group to target a specific audience while a second group focuses on a different grouping.

The steps for getting ad groups ready are as follows:

1. Go to the Campaigns section and click on the Ad Groups tab.

2. *Enter a name for the ad group.*

3. Enter the specific videos you want to use in the ad group.

4. Choose whether the ads will be ones listed on YouTube searches or in-stream ads that play before videos. You can only use one ad format at a time.

5. *Enter the bid amount and budgeting information you wish to use plus the targeting options.*

6. Save the ad group.

Your ad groups can be diverse and organized in many forms. You can produce one ad group that introduces people to your business. Another could feature videos that are for people who are already familiar with your brand. Keeping separate groups ready ensures you will establish ads that target different groups of people. You need to use different campaigns with multiple ad groups that work for everyone-ones who know who you are, those who want to know more, and the people who have no idea who you are.

Promote Your Channel

You may be thinking that this entire book is mostly about promoting your channel, and you'd be right, but promoting is actually an option on YouTube where you can spend money as well. YouTube gives everyone the option to "promote" their channel on the site. This means that you actually pay YouTube a sum of money and one or multiple of your videos will show up in special places on the website. If you've ever clicked on a video and an "ad" played beforehand, and it was more like a separate video than an ad, this was a promoted video. Promoting gives you the opportunity to have your video played before other people's videos of a related content, or shows up more commonly on recommended videos lists. It may put your video in the related videos section of other videos that aren't yours as well. Obviously, this is a really good option for spreading your channel around and gaining subscribers. There's not an easier way to promote your channel than this option. The question ultimately becomes whether the number of subscribers you gain is worth the amount of money you have to spend getting YouTube to promote your work. You have to have funds to pay for this promotion and this means having enough money budgeted in your company's marketing funds or having enough in your personal banking account to do so. If you believe the amount of fans you gain is worth the price, then it may be the best way to go.

If your YouTube channel is meant to promote your business to begin with, this is definitely a good option. Even if the promotion doesn't add that many followers to your YouTube channel, it still may add new customers to your business. This may be cheaper than running more conventional advertisement campaigns on television or other platforms.

As mentioned earlier, the demographics that watch YouTube regularly are considerably younger, making advertising there a great way to attract a young and more hip customer base.

Just make sure that the content of your videos is not too controversial or inappropriate, as especially lately, YouTube has not been so keen on spreading these types of videos around their website, as it affects their advertisement options with other companies. If you have controversial content, it is still possible to promote, but it is recommended to use your least brazen videos to use this feature.

Chapter 11 Snapchat Marketing

Why use Snapchat?

This messaging app has come a long way, and it is estimated that it receives about 10 billion views a day and that the average user visits their Snapchat up to 18 times a day. So, what are the benefits of using Snapchat as a marketing tool?

1. No pressure

Unlike the early days of Facebook where most people worried about updating their statuses, Snapchat is relatively easy going. You can put as little or as much content as you want to and there's no pressure in that. Many businesses are too slow in acclimatizing themselves into Snapchat marketing, which has contributed to the laidback attitude toward the app. However, as video is set to become the biggest conduit of content, overtaking text, marketers will finally awaken to the utility of apps such as Snapchat. This app attracts more than three times YouTube's views. Even though marketers haven't totally warmed up to it, there are a ton of early birds who are minting money by marketing through the app.

2. Gain exposure

This app boasts an extremely active audience. Comprised mostly of young people, the average user checks their profile about 18 times a day. This means the engagement level is quite solid. If you'd craft a marketing message that users can identify with, you'd obviously gain a lot of engagement. Snapchat has also made it easy for people on other platforms to follow you. Once you create your account, you may update your other social media accounts with its QR code to let other people follow you. Unlike other platforms that seem to be hitting a plateau, Snapchat is on the rise and is set to break records in the near future.

3. Real-Time Marketing

Snapchat utilizes powerful structures and technology. One of the features is known as stories, where users get to watch time-limited videos. The latest feature allows users to send a screenshot of their watching stories to their friends. Marketers can take advantage of this feature by announcing discounts to whomever that watches the stories and brings out proof of the same at the store. As a video content site, Snapchat is at the forefront of ushering a new era, where video content trumps any other type of content. You can create engaging videos and upload them on your Snapchat and then offer incentives in order to garner the views.

4. Target locations

Snapchat allows marketers to interact with their followers not just on a real-time basis but also basing on location. Marketers can take advantage of this feature to promote their businesses and welcome their customers into intimate spaces of their lives. A marketing strategy that has a personal touch is always far more effective than cold words floating through the vast internet. When you have real-time communication with your followers, it becomes much easier to inspire them, educate them, and even bring out their tears. And as we know, emotion is the best prelude to conversion.

5. *Build a community*

Snapchat gives you the capability to form a community of believers around your brand. Such kind of thinking is what got Apple Inc to where it is today. Through Snapchat, you can establish a real-time connection with your followers, and get them to see what your brand is all about. Don't be quick to hard sell them as you may lose your genuineness. It's far much better to have the backing of a community as opposed to one person because they can spread the word around about your brand and products. A community inspires you even to create a better brand and feature-rich products. As they say, "Two hands are better than one," which is to say, your community can really chip in with ideas and suggestions. Your customers are goldmines of ideas. If you just give them a platform and a chance to speak frankly, they would open you up to many possibilities that you never once imagined. As a marketer, you must begin by accepting that you don't have all the answers and that when you hear of a good idea from some other person, you will have the courage to qualify that idea, and not trash it out of envy.

6. Less competition

For the majority of businesses, they are focused on sourcing leads from Twitter, Facebook, and Instagram. Most of them haven't caught up to the new wave of excitement around Snapchat. The earlier you start marketing your brand on Snapchat, the better for you. You will gain much more insight and practical tips, and by the time most businesses discover the magic of Snapchat, you will be some sort of Snapchat marketing legend, optimizing your campaigns in such a fashion that you spend least amounts of money to gain the most profit. With less competition, you have the perfect opportunity to test out various marketing styles and understand what really works for you.

7. High fun element

With most social media networks, the interaction is pretty basic and limited to text. But Snapchat creates an environment of fun by letting users share photos and videos in real time. With more fun, people loosen up, and the conversations become natural. This app enables marketers to free up their time without necessarily forgetting about their business. For instance, if you go away on holiday, you can keep posting random clips on Snapchat just to engage your followers. This is no time to hard sell, but rather a time to enjoy a pleasant moment with your followers.

8. Let your personality shine

Some people are too charismatic and have fun personalities. If you are such, then Snapchat is a great tool for boosting your conversions. Research shows that we tend to buy from people whom we like and trust. With a fun personality, people would no doubt be drawn to you, and it would boost their engagement with your brand, which would culminate into increased sales and brand visibility.

9. The value of trends

Use Snapchat to get your audience hooked on trending matters. If you want to be looked upon as a thought leader in your industry, you must be aware of all the trends and possess a deep and unique insight. You must have social currency. And when you attain the image of a thought leader, you earn people's trust, which eventually leads to a high conversion rate.

Snapchat symbols

❤️ This symbol appears next to a friend's name when you have both sent each other the most snaps.

💕 This symbol indicates a very tight friendship.

😬 The grimace shows you and another person are sharing a close friend.

🔥 When you have been exchanging snaps with another person for days on end.

⌛ When this symbol appears next to a friend's name, it means your Snap-streak is coming to an end.

🎂 This emoji shows up when your friend is celebrating their birthday.

Organic Snap-chat marketing

If you don't want to spend money, or don't have any money to spend, you can always expand your follower base organically and rely on them for revenue. Snapchat may be populated with extremely young people at present, but it is definitely poised to take over as video content becomes the dominant form of content consumption. It is in your best interests to get started promoting your brand on Snapchat.

Tell good stories

We are in 2019, but still, the tenets of a good story remain the same as far back in prehistory era. In order to attract a bigger fan base, you have to post exciting stories on your Snapchat. The following tips should help you tell good stories:

- Keep their eyes moving: as you go on with whatever you are saying or recording, try to shift your followers' angles and make them look around, it adds to the experience.
- Play with the features: Snapchat is an incredibly feature-rich app, just go ahead and play with those features and see how it goes. Use emojis, 3D stickers, filters, and geo-filters.
- Be concise: don't take a whole one-minute standing in the same boring position and saying a lot of nothing and expect to excite your followers. Brevity is the soul of wit. Be brief, but not so brief that meaning is lost.

Collaborate with others

You stand to gain a lot by collaborating with other industry players. Approach someone with a higher following on Snapchat and suggest that you do something together. This should be like a habit of yours. The more you collaborate with other people, the more cross-promotion will take place, and you will finally go viral.

Be responsive

Don't let the few thousand followers you have balloon your ego. If your loyal fans are sending you Snaps saying how cool they think you are, reply back and even give them a shout out. Your fans are always watching how you treat them.

Be consistent

It doesn't matter how great your first twenty stories were if you stopped doing it, if you stopped doing it consistently, you would slowly fall through the cracks into no man's land. You don't want that to happen. There will be bad days, of course. But have the courage to face those bad days so that you can have a reason to celebrate the good days.

Paid Snapchat marketing

Snapchat ads are tailored to help business owners reach their marketing goals by interacting with a young and super engaging audience. The advertisements are displayed between friends' stories and the content curated by Snapchat. If a Snap-chatter is interested in an ad, they can swipe up in order to fulfill the call to action, which might be watching a longer video, reading an article or installing an app.

Pixel

It's basically an application embedded in your site that collects data about visitors' actions and behaviors.

Geo-filters

This tool helps advertisers target audiences in specific locations.

Lenses

Lenses are extremely popular among Snap-chatters as they integrate augmented reality. They use facial recognition technology to transform images.

Context Cards

Aimed at enticing users to click on the links, context cards add more info about a company into the ads.

Deep Links

These are links within an app that link out to other apps.

Snapchat Discover Ads

These ads cost $50000 per day and are obviously reserved for the high-budget companies. Your content is placed at the top of user Discover pages.

Common errors to avoid

Just as it is with other social media networks, there are considerable pitfalls you are at risk of falling into while marketing on Snapchat. These are some of the errors that you should be aware of and desist from:

1. Your stories are too long

If you post long stories, people might be discouraged from clicking. There's nothing wrong with taking your time to say whatever you want to. But then you should use a platform such as YouTube as it is suited for such kind of content. Snapchat users might be extremely active on the platform, but also they are restless. People don't want to have to watch an especially long story as it keeps them back from watching other Snaps that they consider fun. Perhaps the only time it's acceptable to post long stories is when you are making major announcements, not when you are promoting something.

2. Your stories are too short

If it is not okay to post long stories, would short stories do the trick? NO. If your story is so short that you don't communicate anything, then it is worse than even a long story. Always ensure that you provide sufficient context in order for the message to be passed across. Make sure that you are posting enough snaps that your story has a clear narrative and yet concise, and to make your story memorable and worthy use text, emojis and narration. The secret of a good story comes down to combining the features, letting your charisma shine, and ensuring that it is just the right length.

3. Posting Too Frequently

Another mistake that users might make is posting too frequently, forcing your followers to put up with your content. Less is more. Have some breaks to it. But if you are an ever-present fixture, you will slowly and irreversibly lose your shine, and finally, everyone will get tired of you and tell you as much. On Twitter, you might get away with shooting a new post every two hours, but on Snapchat it would be an incredibly bad idea. Focus on creating quality stories and uploading between evenly spaced out intervals. As a marketer, you may upload stories even twice or thrice in a week.

4. Failing to include a call to action

A call to action is an invitation for the user to perform some specific action. If you create a perfect story about the benefits of your new product and fail to ask your followers to click on the link, you have omitted a call to action. It might seem simple, but it is incredibly effective. As a marketer, you are a figure of authority, and you are supposed to guide your babies (followers) into taking the appropriate actions. Of course, some followers will figure out that they need to click on the call to action button, but then there are others who couldn't care less.

5. You're too boring and predictable

If you recycle a joke two times we will forgive you, but not a third time! The problem is not many people have taken the time to develop their personalities and become charismatic — also, not many people like researching before sitting down to come up with content. You will find that the average Snapchat user just starts talking into their phone without planning anything at all. That's the reason why it's hard to come across a consistently fun person to watch. Everyone appears to sound funny at the start, but then their well of ideas runs out, and they don't get out of their comfort zone, so they start to recycle old content, faintly at first, and then full blown with no trace of embarrassment. As a marketer, you must only post stories when you have something of value. Don't do it for the sake.

6. Having no sense of direction

You will hardly achieve anything without a clear direction. If today you are talking about women's clothes, and tomorrow you are talking about alternative medicine, and the day after tomorrow about ghosts, it shows that you have no clear direction. People won't take you seriously. Post content that is strictly tied to your brand. Of course, you can introduce fun aspects, narrations, and all other sweet little things, but ultimately you must steer your account with congruency. This is what will make you stand out and attract the audience that you have been seeking.

7. Not promoting your account

If your strategy is to post awesome content consistently with the hopes of going viral, that strategy might take forever. But to jumpstart your followers, you may need to promote your account. Start by telling your friends to follow you on Snapchat. And then get into sponsored content.

- Create a snap ad: this is a half-minute video that will appear alongside relevant content, and it will help you gain more followers.
- Choose sponsored geo-filters
- Offer interactive content

8. Posting at the wrong time

A snap appears for a few seconds before snuffing out and disappearing into the big jungle that is the internet. Knowing this, you must post stories at the appropriate times. This is when your target audience is most active.

9. Not using the localization feature

The localization feature is very critical. Users can leverage this feature to draw in people who are within the same area. This feature can help people take the conversation from the internet into a physical one. Sadly, a lot of people underutilize this feature, or not use it at all.

Chapter 12 LinkedIn

LinkedIn can be a profitable hotspot for web-based systems administration publicizing. It is definitely not hard to use and free, with in excess of 468 million people.

This is the place people plan to sort out, become progressively familiar with different associations, and develop their own one of a kind business circles. Despite what organization or thing a LinkedIn page addresses, it puts an individual, yet capable face on any association.

Coming up next are the best different ways LinkedIn can be used to grab attention from this group, and produce quality leads for your business.

Solicitation Recommendations

As the business person, when an individual profile has been set up and a couple of partners and delegates have been developed in the framework, it's basic to make a couple of request from these relation-ship for proposals. Solicitation that satisfied customers set up a few kind words, or solicitation that a careful agent do similarly. Repeat these exercises as habitually as could be normal considering the present situation, with the true objective to get the best reviews for your business and for your master works out. This is a basic bit of the collaboration that is significant on LinkedIn – people look for analysis on their things and organizations – get input (especially if it's certain).

React with Recommendations

Since internet organizing is set up in the relationship between people, it's furthermore comparably as basic to give out reviews and recommendations to accomplices and to clients. Be liberal and veritable. If a proposition is sincere, it will show up. Display how invigorating laborers are, and endorse appropriately. Afresh, this is a bit of the association that is basic in web based systems administration exhibiting with the ultimate objective to create leads dependent on trust and proclivity.

Make a Brand Group

An individual framework is unimaginable, and is basic on LinkedIn for showing the validity of the association, yet it won't reach past that orchestrate. Rather than spamming and sending requests self-assertively, which is significantly incapable (and too many spam standards can get a record confined on LinkedIn, fortuitously) for quality lead age; make a brand assembling and keep the option checked to "demonstrate this get-together in the Groups Directory" with the true objective to accomplish a much progressively broad framework.

Remember, LinkedIn has in excess of 468 million people. There are various people who may be enthusiastic about joining bundles for any number of topics; everything from SEO advancing, to exploratory composition. Thusly, make a social occasion that joins drawing in catchphrases in the title, or an average depiction to tell people what kind of get-together it is. At the point when the social event is completely operational, keep it invigorated with relevant focuses and mull over open trade. Partake, continually recollecting that the correspondence is the indispensable part to online life displaying.

Use Regular Profile Updates

Normal and relentless updates of a profile will keep it in the news channel, and can get eagerness from affiliations. Clearly, one wouldn't care to make profile revives that are pointless – that will simply serve to trouble relationship in case they have to consistently watch it in their news sources. In this manner, guarantee that they are proper updates, and take care of self-evident expertise.

Use an Image to Create an Image

It's a keen idea to have whatever number individual contacts as could sensibly be normal on both the LinkedIn profile page, and furthermore in the brand's social occasion page. Remember the 5 P's – exchange an exquisite, capable individual profile picture – it incorporates a human touch and urges relationship with interface and be destroyed in to one's profile. The other spot an image is fundamental is on the brand's social occasion page. Use the association's logo and put the business' best foot forward.

As an issue of first significance, online life displaying, paying little mind to what site, is about the joint effort among association and leads – between people – so exploit it by interfacing! A specialist atmosphere is continually basic, anyway significantly more so for the LinkedIn culture. Contact current customers, get endorsed to their allies, and tap into the more critical market through a brand gathering. This is an unprecedented technique to start on LinkedIn – it's straightforward and conceivable, and takes a base proportion of time concerning the publicist.

Chapter 13 Social Media Marketing Mistakes to Avoid

When you get on social media, it is important that you understand that your success is not guaranteed just because you created an account and shared a few posts. When it comes to social media, many businesses are trying to reach the same audience as you are, so you need to make sure that you stand out in the crowd. The market is far from being "tapped out," but if you come onto a platform without knowing how to use it effectively, you are quickly going to get overlooked as your audience favors brands who come in with a strategy.

In this chapter, you are going to learn what risks to avoid when using social media in general to ensure that you are not wasting your time using the wrong growth strategies online. You will learn what mistakes to avoid on each specific platform later, but for now, it is important that you understand the general risks to avoid so that you can have a massive impact online from day one.

Overstretching Yourself
Every single social media platform comes with a learning curve that you will need to endure in order to discover to master the platform and begin earning a high return on your social media marketing efforts. Regardless of whether or not you have already been on the platform, if you are not yet used to using that platform for marketing, you will need to learn how to adjust your approach and ensure that it is optimized for marketing so that you can increase your earnings. When you are looking to use social media for marketing, it is important that you do not overstretch yourself as this can

lead to not having the required attention to endure each learning curve and actually put that platform to use.

In order to ensure that you are not overstretching yourself, start by being honest about how much time you have each day to master your social media. If you only have a small amount of time per day or a few hours per week, it may be ideal to start out on the platform that is most likely to earn you an income. Then grow from there so that you are giving yourself enough time to thoroughly understand each platform. Once you have understood that first platform, then you can go ahead and start branching out to others so that you can master those as well.

Although you may want to grow big online quickly, it is important to understand where the balance lies when it comes to your growth. That is, it is a lot more productive to go big on one platform at a time, than it is to spread yourself so thin that none of your platforms gain traction and you miss the mark on every social media site you try. You will find that you master each platform and grow a lot more quickly this way, making it easier for you to start generating great success online relatively quickly.

Spending Time on the Wrong Platforms
Another big risk that you might make online is spending time on the wrong platforms or targeting the wrong parts of the platforms. If you are not directing your time and attention properly, you can quickly get drawn into taking actions that are not productive to your overall goal, which leaves you at risk of wasting a lot of time and not getting a lot of results.

Just because you may personally prefer one platform over another, or you may personally feel like one is better suited to your business compared to another, does not mean that this is actually the best choice. You need to go where your audience is and position yourself directly in front of them, or you are going to find yourself falling flat on your face online.

This way, you can ensure that you are focusing entirely on areas that will support you, rather than areas that will not.

Not Embracing the Learning Curve

When people get on social media, one of the biggest disservices they can do for themselves and their business is to fail to embrace the learning curve that comes with being on social media for marketing purposes. If you get on social media and fail to embrace the learning curve or try to do everything your way, you are going to find rather quickly that this is ineffective and that you are going to struggle to succeed online. While you certainly do need to embrace authenticity and freedom of expression online, failing to understand the basic concepts of how to get seen and heard online will only result in you struggling to grow your business.

The learning curve can take a few days, a few weeks, or even a few months depending on how much time you have to invest in social media and what you are doing to learn about the learning curve itself. If you want to accelerate this time, reading books like this one and paying attention to regular algorithm changes, new releases, and platform updates is a great opportunity to make sure that you are learning everything there is to know as quickly as possible. Aside from consuming the information, you also need to practice putting it to work online so that you can ensure that you are aware of both what the information is and how it works in practice. The more you read, learn, and integrate social media strategies online, the faster you will be at getting your business out there and for an online impact.

That being said, make sure that you are not going too quickly online, either. If you change your strategy too frequently, no matter what platform you are on, you will find yourself struggling to stay seen because people will grow confused with what it is that you are trying to achieve. You need to be willing to give each strategy the time required to allow it to accumulate reasonable results based on your efforts so that you can determine whether or not it worked, how it could have been improved, and what can be maintained when you start adjusting your strategies.

Blending Personal with Professional

Finally, even if you are running a personal brand, you need to be cautious about how much you blend your personal life with your professional life. Attempting to blend your personal and professional lives too much can result in you oversharing online and muddying the face of your business. You need to be cautious when it comes to building a brand, especially a personal one. You must ensure that you are not sharing information that could result in you taking away from the reputation or clarity of your business. In other words, even if you have a personal brand, keep your professional and personal lives separate to avoid having personal information leak into your business and destroy your professionalism.

Even if you are well-meaning, there will be many parts of your personal life that are simply not on-brand and, if you share them, it could result in you being seen as confusing or unprofessional. At the end of the day, even if you are sharing a personal brand, there are certain parts of your life that people simply do not want to read about or heed. The people who are following you will be more interested in the stuff that relates to them, or problems they may be facing, over anything else. This is not because people do not care about you, but because you are positioning yourself and your personal brand as a business. You need to be prepared to behave like a business.

If you do want to have a personal online platform, make sure that you keep your personal accounts private and separate from your business accounts. You can always share your business life with your personal friends but refrain from sharing your personal life with your business connections unless it in some way makes sense to your business. For example, if you are starting a fashion blog, you can share about fashion topics with your professional network but refrain from sharing about your love life or relationships unless it in some way can be tied into your outfit. If you were to wear a cute outfit on a date, for example, you could share this, but do not share about your hardships or troubles that your relationship may be facing online as this will only lead to you being seen as unprofessional. If you want to be seen as a professional business and have the opportunity to do business like a professional, you need to behave like a professional online at all times.

Conclusion

The next step is to begin researching other successful personal brands and why they interest you. Take the time to get an understanding of why they are successful. Then go on to complete the personal branding foundation checklist, realizing what you have to offer the world and how you can utilize what makes you unique and valuable to begin a long and fulfilling career. Continue to research possible mentors and idols, as well as new or innovative techniques and brands that you could admire and incorporate into your own efforts. Remember to take an honest and accurate gauge of the resources that are available to you, and use them with care and responsibility. When beginning to build your personal brand, remember to always be yourself and make an active and purposeful effort to curate a unique, styled, and marketable brand and image that will sell your persona and skills. No one else can be Martha Stewart, and no one else can be YOU.

www.ingramcontent.com/pod-product-compliance
Lightning Source LLC
Chambersburg PA
CBHW070619220526
45466CB00001B/59